GUILTY
PLEASURES

PRAISE FOR GUILTY PLEASURES

"This book depicts the true essence of a woman in search of peace, love, and happiness, and all the dynamics she encounters on her mission." –Breeze, An avid reader

"I enjoyed it…it was sexy." –Thomas Green, Author of *Courting Miss Thang*

"Sonya Harris has crafted a novel that encourages one to look within…*Guilty Pleasures* is an enjoyable read that truly lives up to its title." –RAWSISTAZ Reviewers

"Reading *Guilty Pleasures* again was like reading it for the first time. It had me feeing like I knew these people or could understand exactly their pain." –Actress LaTamra Smith

"*Guilty Pleasures* invites you into a world of revelation, love, and reality.
This is a novel to read." –Saadia Coleman, Educator

ALSO BY SONYA HARRIS

My Body Is Calling
978-0-9754458-2-2

Visit www.sonyaharris.com for information, updates, and
events.
Like me on Facebook: author_sonyaharris
Follow me on Twitter: @author_sonya

GUILTY PLEASURES

A Novel

Sonya Harris

Sayha Publishing

The ego doesn't know that the source of all energy is within you, so it seeks it outside. –Eckhart Tolle

Dedicated to Self-Awareness.
Knowing who you are
is more important than
who you are pretending to be.

CONTENTS

PROLOGUE

Wet bar dry to the bone, late night at the upscale Millennium Hotel, a respected, married lawyer worked my wallet-chasing friend Keisha so hard between the sheets, he passed out.

While his cheating ass lay recuperating, Keisha stole crisp $100 bills from his wallet and then embarked on a speed-dialing frenzy, burning minutes on her married lover's trendy cell phone. She plugged numbers found in his contact list until she scored big with his wife. Keisha sat dipping leftover strawberries in whipped cream before playing her evil game of kiss-and-tell. The consensus of a mistress being a home wrecker has a tinge of truth to it.

"Hello Mrs. Home Alone." Keisha giggled. "Do you know where your husband is?"

"And, who would like to know?" asked the wife.

"Who I am is not important," Keisha scoffed.

"The hell it isn't. Now, if you know something about my husband, please tell me, or I'll call the police."

"Involving the law wouldn't be wise. Let me save you the embarrassment of a public scandal. Hold the line so your husband can tell you who I am."

Just as Keisha was about to turn around and shake Gordon awake, he snatched the phone, slapped one hand over her mouth, disconnected the call, and yelled, "Bitch!" He then knocked Keisha upside her head with his heavy hand, sending her crashing against the wall. She was woozy after impact. The fact that she had polished off two bottles of top shelf champagne also wasn't helping her balance.

When Keisha slumped to the floor Gordon climbed on top of her. He grabbed her neck with one hand and tried to ram the other hand deep into her pussy.

"Do you wanna know what it feels like to be fucked over?" He shouted forcing his hand deeper inside her. "I warned you about the consequences of involving my wife in our business."

"Gordon, please stop. It hurts. I'm sorry." Keisha groaned as she tried to squirm away. "It was only a prank. I wasn't gonna tell her about us. I swear I wasn't."

He slipped his hand out of her and joined it with the other wrapped around her throat. "You lying little tramp."

A thundering knock pounded the door. "Mr. Upshaw, is everything all right in there? Guests are complaining about the noise," whispered a male voice from the outside.

Gordon jabbed a finger in Keisha's face. "Not one word. Not *one!*" He scrambled to collect the money from the floor, covered himself in a complimentary bathrobe, and then opened the door. "Do you mind? I'm fucking my wife." He said, and then slapped the crisp $100 bills in the palm of the hotel concierge, who knew of his illicit affairs.

"Mr. Upshaw I'm sorry."

"Don't apologize. Go away!" Gordon said, slamming the door to resume punishing Keisha.

First, he pumped anger, power, and disrespect inside of her, building up to an entitled climax. After pulling out, he removed the condom, and then rammed his slimy dick in her mouth. Keisha sucked his authority against her will. Gordon then pissed superiority in her mouth causing Keisha to gag and choke. Afterward, he picked up her cell phone.

"What are you doing? Give me my phone." Keisha shouted.

"I'm about to show you who writes the rules and how the game is played." Adding insult to injury, Gordon then phoned the front desk to report Keisha as an uninvited guest.

"I can't believe you're being petty because I called your wife."

"That won't happen again, will it? Now get dressed."

A few minutes later Keisha was unceremoniously escorted out by hotel security as the concierge taunted, "You're not his first trick and you won't be his last."

Unrepentant, Keisha flipped him the birdie.

Raindrops falling gently against the skylight above my bed was the sound I heard before drifting off to sleep last night.

Waking up, I felt under the sheets for the television remote control, usually tucked away in the pillowcase for easy access. Instead, I found my night scarf, and the bobby pins that were supposed to keep it secured on my head.

I rolled out of bed, and slipped into my Tweety Bird slippers. I sauntered to the bathroom, pulled the chain, took a sanitizing shower, and beautified my body with cocoa butter and Vaseline for the really dry spots. I definitely inherited Daddy's dry skin. I then ventured downstairs to brew a fresh cup of coffee in the pot still filled with yesterday's grounds.

While I fumbled around in the pantry for the coffee filters, my doorbell chimed. "Fur Elise" played softly through the house like a soothing wind chime.

I was reluctant to approach the door but decided to answer the bell even though it went against my Rule of Visiting: Call before you come, which included my mother Claire.

I opened the door a crack, then wider to study the tiny turquoise box sitting on the front stoop, neatly wrapped with its signature white ribbon.

"Hmm. What do we have here?" I said, as I examined the address label. The postmark was stamped "local", so it was mailed in Boston.

I looked up and down the street but didn't see anyone. That left me confused. And I knew it hadn't come from my on again, off-again boyfriend Andy who doesn't have the kind of class to know that big things came in small packages.

I have a history of attracting jive players like Andy who are only capable of picking out greeting cards with sappy words they can't express to me themselves. For that reason, I thought the deliveryman must've mistaken my address for another Romeo's Juliet.

I double-checked the address label. The only sign of a name was the "R" written in the sender's field. I then checked for a sender's address but found only a P.O. Box. Whoever sent it lived within walking distance because we had the same zip code. While I stood there wondering who'd sent the box, my neighbor Ritchie opened his door and announced himself with his usual effusive energy.

"Miss Thing! He shouted. "A hot delivery man was ringing your bell. I swear he looked like he stepped out of a calendar centerfold." As usual, Ritchie was exuberant with his graphic details and kept going. "Miss Thing, he was a gorgeous, oiled down specimen of a man. Whew!" Ritchie fanned himself.

"I wanted to touch every sizzling inch of his athletic body." Ritchie then did his best Diana Ross impression as he sang, "I want muscles, all over, all over..."

His theatrics were high in the I'm–so-lonely-zone, and with good cause. It had been almost a year since his lover Paul left him for a bisexual man.

Ignoring Ritchie, I picked up the box, and went back inside. Like a fierce tiger destroys her prey, I tore into the package and rummaged through the tissue paper and pulled out an embossed business card. The writing on the back of the card read: "Free consultation for a pretty woman." I turned over the card and it was for the address of a Dr. Rosen, who was— of all things—a shrink!

Completely baffled, I could only think of one local person with the initial "R" and the audacity to do something like this. Ritchie! *But why on Earth would Ritchie refer me to a therapist?* It didn't make sense. He didn't know enough about my private life to make such a bold assumption.

The ringing telephone interrupted my thoughts. I went into the living room and picked it up.

"Your dime, my time, which one will be wasted?"

"Simone. Let me tell you about last night's drama." Keisha stated.

"Let me guess, your married man's wife almost caught you fucking her husband."

"Close. Gordon went ballistic because I crank-called his wife after putting it on him something fierce at the Millennium Hotel." Keisha casually admitted giggling.

"You're not gonna be laughing when his wife stomps you beyond recognition. You best leave that married man alone if you know what's good for you."

"His wife needs to learn how to satisfy her unfaithful husband before stepping to me with hurt feelings."

"Keisha, most wives and girlfriends blame the other woman, so you better be careful filling in the gaps before you find yourself begging for mercy in court, or worse catch an incurable sexually transmitted disease."

"It's not like I'm having sex with multiple partners and Gordon and I practice safe-sex."

"Keisha, sexing a married man is risky business, not to mention reckless sex. Besides his wife and you, you have no idea who else he's sleeping with."

"So what. He's good to me. I'm good to him. We have an arrangement that I enjoy. And it sure beats dating single, broke, bums."

"Then why are you jeopardizing something you enjoy by involving his wife? Do you want him for yourself?"

"No. I'm satisfied with no commitment as long as he keeps my feet looking pretty in designer shoes and money in my bank account."

"You can do all that yourself."

"I know but I love living on the edge with Gordon. Since when have you known me to date anything but financially stable married men?"

"Never. Anyway, let me tell you what I found at my front door this morning."

"Who, Andy stalking you for make-up sex?"

"Cute, but no. A turquoise box."

"As in from Tiffany's?" Keisha squealed. "Welcome to the Get Money Club! When'd you hook a seven-figure man?"

"Hardly. I've got plenty of my own cash in the bank. Wanna compare bank statements? Or should we wait until your latest married wallet gets over your trifling shenanigans and makes a deposit?"

"Blah, blah, blah, Miss Independent."

"Don't 'blah' me. Listen, I've got a bone to pick with Ritchie. We can talk about your married-man problems later."

Before Keisha could say another word I hung up and dialed Ritchie's number. Though good-looking, confident, and without a doubt, a people person, Ritchie has been a bachelor since Paul, his domestic partner, abandoned him. With no friends or relatives close by, his holidays were often spent alone, or at work putting in double-time creating marketing campaigns for small start-up businesses. Homophobic men shunned him and most women found his proud-to-be-gay theatrics annoying, but not me.

If Ritchie were attracted to women, I'd be all over him like cheese on grits for his kitchen skills. But according to Ritchie, he was 100 percent gay-for-life, strictly dickly. I could prance around in only a thong and he would politely point out the cellulite and refer me to his personal trainer. Ritchie is one man I couldn't turn on even if a million bucks were strapped to my ass. Though obnoxiously flamboyant, Ritchie meant well and his heart was as big as Texas. I was his friend, no matter who he chose to love, and I couldn't wait to hear what his madness was all about.

"Single and looking. Name your price." Ritchie answered on the second ring.

At first, I thought about pretending to be his fantasy deliveryman but then decided against it because he really was "single and looking."

"It's Simone, and I would like to know—"

"Miss Thing! Thank goodness it's you. I need to talk to somebody. I don't want to suffer in silence anymore."

Before I could light into Ritchie for his unsolicited psychiatric referral, a tidal wave of emotions spilled through the receiver.

"What's going on? You were just excited about the mailman, and now you're all worked up."

"Seeing that good looking man reminded me of Paul and how lonely I've been since he left me. I want to call him but every time I find the nerve, all the nasty things he did remind me why I asked him to leave."

"Nasty things like what?"

"Don't judge me for over sharing, but Paul sometimes slapped me around and he once smeared his shit in my face."

"He did what?"

"You heard me. We considered counseling, but Paul's idea of therapy was finding sexual healing in another man's bed."

"Ritchie, somebody had to go, so maybe you should be relieved that Paul left. If what you're saying is true, then your exit point should have been the moment he smeared you with his shit. I hope you filed assault charges. Did you?"

"No."

"So you chose to suffer partner abuse in silence because of pride?"

"He didn't draw blood. Plus he left."

"Did you take back your keys?"

"No Miss Thing." Ritchie answered with a touch of irritation.

"Then I hope you changed your locks."

"Have you counted my locks? Hiring a Locksmith would be too expensive. But it's not necessary. Paul is gone for good. I even helped him pack."

"Are you sure?"

"Seriously, it's over. I got tired of him beating on me."
Ritchie snapped his fingers and said, "A *Divo* can only take so
much."

"Okay, *Divo*, if you say so. After today no more complaining. I've got my own life to manage."

"I'm just happy you got rid of that character Andy. Thank the
Lord for small miracles because he was tired if you ask me. In
fact, he was so tired he made me sleepy." Ritchie yawned loudly
over the phone. "See, I'm yawning just thinking about that fool."

"Oh, so now Mr. Vulnerable wants to tell jokes."

"Don't be so sensitive. You know Andy wasn't up to snuff.
You can do better. Get a man with some Benjamins, that's all
I've got to say."

"Ritchie, we've been kind of dating again."

There was a long pause on the line before Ritchie spoke.

"You sneaky slut. Then I advise you to keep that card I
sent. You might need it one day." Ritchie finally said.

"That was actually why I was calling. I don't recall asking
you for mental health advice."

"You didn't have to. The depth of your eyes tells me your
drama is thick."

"Ritchie Allen Poe stop analyzing me and get a better handle on your own shitty problems."

"It's been handled. Paul's not here anymore."

"Well, good for you. Now if you don't mind, I've got chores
to do."

"Don't trash the card."

"I will." I said laughing and then hung up still confused.
So, he did send the card. But, why? I've got my life under control. At
least that's what I wanted to believe.

1

I LOVE ME

Two years later, dark and gloomy, I walked into Dr. Rosen's office shouldering burdens and pains. I'd had it up to my eyebrows; everything came to a halt that day.

I remember my first session with Dr. Rosen as clearly as if it was yesterday. I was at a breaking point. A terrible argument with Andy, my sister Susan's drug relapse, and a worse week at work pushed me to schedule an emergency appointment with Dr. Rosen. Luckily I'd kept the card that Ritchie had sent me.

Dr. Rosen quietly guided me to his office. I entered a broken and emotionally battered woman. The special chair, as I liked to call the Director's chair, was positioned near the window. Next to it was a maple credenza, on top of which sat a box of Kleenex, a water pitcher, disposable cups and napkins.

That day, I decided to sit in the special chair with the words I Love Me printed on the back, instead of the chaise lounge, partly because I was determined to make progress over the next five weeks of sessions. Sitting in the chair I felt in charge, and much more at ease. I even smiled.

Dr. Rosen sat in his executive-style chair, ready to jot down whatever I rattled off in response to his questions. He began, "I see you chose the Director's chair as your choice of seating today. Can you tell me why you chose to sit in the Director's chair, and not the chaise lounge?"

I was glad that he'd noticed something significant about my actions without me having to make noise, jump up and down, and ball my eyes out in frustration. I stalled to collect myself before answering. I repositioned the chair so my back was facing the window to keep my mind from wandering. I wiggled, found a comfortable spot, and responded.

"I wanted to feel in control, in charge for once. Plus, you didn't encourage me to sit anywhere else."

"That's good." Dr. Rosen said with positive reinforcement. "Now that you've made a decision on your own, do you think it was necessary for someone else to encourage you to do something that might make you feel better?"

"No, and besides, I've been trying to think more about myself, that's why I'm here."

"Ms. Miller. Life is all about the way we feel inside."

"And today, I feel great because I'm here. Please call me Simone."

"Okay, if that's what you prefer. Simone," he said cautiously. "You're even smiling a great deal, and expressed your desire to execute some of your goals that have been tabled. I especially want to applaud your decision to finish your undergraduate degree. Education is very important. However, I caution you not to move too quickly. Making rash changes sometimes create impatience and disappointment."

"I know. One day at a time. Don't take on more than I can handle. Expect setbacks and grow from experience." I recited.

Dr. Rosen smiled, "And put *you* first."

Five sessions later, I had finally come full circle with the discontentment in my life. My mental state of mind was well on its way to being cleansed of social and emotional drama.

At my last appointment, Dr. Rosen handed me a silver gift bag, overflowing with pastel tissue paper. "Please accept this small token for not giving up on becoming a better you."

"Oh, Dr. Rosen, you didn't have to buy me anything."

"No worries. It's what I do for all of my patients who stay the course."

"Thank you." I said taking the gift. Inside was a book titled *Codependent No More* by Melody Beattie. Reading it became a high priority on my Bucket List.

At the end of what I prayed was my last session, Dr. Rosen and I shook hands, exchanged pleasantries and said good-bye. I left hoping to never return under the humiliating circumstances that sent me there in the first place.

With the help of Dr. Rosen's warmth and expertise, I was well on my way to discovering something I never felt or imagined in my wildest dreams: self-love. The healthiest decision I made at that point in my life was not throwing away Dr. Rosen's card, for once I felt like I was finally dealing with a man of substance.

After my appointment, I grabbed a handful of his cards for family, and hurting friends who were badly in need of help. On the back of each card I wrote, *Face your demons or they will conquer you* and then stuffed them in my journal for safekeeping.

2

SLIPPING THROUGH THE CRACKS

It was the start of summer, and refreshing after a long, blustery winter. I thought the cold days and frigid nights would never end. But they did, one month into spring.

That morning, I woke up to the sweet sound of birds chirping and the swaying of full-bloomed trees in a warm wind. As I planned my agenda for the day, my head throbbed from the Pina Coladas I drank the night before. My hangover was slightly overshadowed by the fact that I still had to pack for my trip to Florida.

The digital numbers on the dusty clock flashed a way too early 6:00 A.M. I knew then to reprioritize my agenda to include dusting furniture before I ran off to be in somebody's wedding.

Instead of cleaning the house top-to-bottom, I reserved energy for the possibility of a roll in the sand with a well-hung Mandingo Warrior. It had been a while since I'd had sex and actually *enjoyed* it. *As horny as I am, Mandingo and I would work up enough sweat to turn sand into a tropical storm,*

I thought. But I quickly got a grip on my libido. During that time, I'd been practicing abstinence. My legs had been closed tight, denying Andy the pleasure of selfishly emptying his balls while also leaving my heart empty.

More importantly, why was I awake? My flight wasn't scheduled to leave Boston until 11:00 A.M. I still had ample time to pack, dress and conduct my home security walk-through.

I didn't have to worry about food spoiling because the refrigerator was practically empty except for a dozen eggs, three half-empty condiment jars, a carton with a sip of orange juice, and frost spillover from the empty freezer. Perishables were the least of my concerns. My eating habits were reduced to boiled eggs, yogurt and a piece of fruit for breakfast, a hearty soup and sandwich lunch, and not-so-healthy Ramen noodles for dinner. I was the epitome of economical living and clearly defined what hand-to-mouth meant on a temp's salary. But I was content with temporary work status because it gave me a time out from the aggravation of office politics.

Slipping out of bed I walked unsteadily to the bathroom. Sunlight filtered through my khaki-colored blinds, making the morning sunrise easy on my eyes.

I moved at an unsteady pace, along the narrow hall, covered with Afro-centric art. A novice drinker, I was no match for Andy during dinner at Quattro's Italian-American Bistro. My low tolerance for alcohol got me cut off after two drinks while seasoned drinker Andy easily threw back several Jack Daniels on the rocks.

My head pounded with every step to the bathroom. Once there, I tripped over the doorsill and landed on the toilet. Uneasy about flying, I stayed put a few more minutes, and prayed for a safe flight.

After using the bathroom, I prepared to lose myself in a soothing shower. When I turned on the faucet, a swollen bruise on my arm caused pain.

"Damn you, Andy!" I cursed him for manhandling me last night when I fought to throw him and his hard penis out of my house. Andy left seething because he couldn't have his way with me.

The hot water quickly steamed up the bathroom. I slipped out of my satin pajamas and examined my face in the mirror above the sink. I saw a bewildered but still beautiful woman, but for how long? "Could everything I cherish: my youth, my spirit, and my mind, slip away before I found love and happiness?" I worried.

The revelation in the mirror weighed heavily on my mind and forced me to question, "Why couldn't I find the love my heart ached for?"

To ease my mind, I constructed a smiley face with bright eyes and a round button nose in the center of the mirror. I could only imagine happiness at such a confusing time in my life. Loving Andy complicated my heart and scattered my brain, leaving me weak and out of touch with my sense of self.

In my moment of sadness, my heart ached for relief. My hangover felt worse. "Damn you, Andy!" I cursed again. I then leaned on my favorite scripture to help me cope: *Let not your heart be troubled and above all else, guard your heart for it is the wellspring of life.*

3

STRUGGLE FOR DIGNITY

Foreplay for Andy was usually a romantic evening out at Quattros, his favorite Italian restaurant. Dinner was his prerequisite for non-committal sex. Our date started out seemingly sweet but concluded on a sour note.

We were seated immediately and our meals came shortly after we ordered. I indulged in crispy fried calamari, which I enjoyed with a bowl of extra spicy salsa on the side. Andy didn't care for squid. He ordered his usual Eggplant Parmesan, which he drowned in grated cheese, and of course cocktails to wash it all down.

In between enjoying our meal and drinks, we told jokes, talked about our day, played under the table footsie, and fondled one another on the sly.

After dinner, a few drinks, and conversation, Andy drove me home. Our child's play took a dramatic adult turn when we arrived at my house. Before I could even unlock the door, Andy cupped my breasts from behind. His rock hard dick was practically in my butt. A swift elbow to his ribs backed him up, but not for long. He advanced on me again, making his play for a sex-fueled nightcap.

In a firm tone I said, "Andy, please, not tonight. I think we've both had a little too much to drink."

"Speak for yourself," he said. "I want some of that sexy pussy between your legs. Come on. Give me what I've been missing for a month now."

"Andy, you're drunk and being disrespectful talking to me like I'm some whore you picked up at a nightclub."

As soon as I said whore, Andy unzipped his zipper, squeezed his manhood, and started panting like a dog. He was in rare form and showing his ass, *literally*. I bet snooping Neighborhood Watch Committee member Miss Bonita was getting an eye full. Her lights went out as soon as the car engine turned off. I feared that Ritchie would pop up and add to our circus show. I quickly stepped inside, and turned to Andy to give him the bad news.

"Sorry. I'm not up for company."

Andy ignored me, pushed open the door and invited himself in. He clearly had an agenda.

Once inside, he dragged me to the couch, bent me over the backrest pulled up my dress, and pinned me down as he tried to force his dick inside me.

"No! Andy, Stop!" I screamed, but he ignored me. His dick was hard, and he was ready to fuck. In the middle of my struggle for dignity, Andy had the nerve to say, "I'm gonna miss you while you're out of town, leave me with a sweet and sexy memory."

There was no reasoning with him. Our power struggle was bound to get worse; we'd been down the road of resistance before. I had one last chance before it was too late. I started crying like a colicky baby. It always worked.

Andy instantly went limp. He then pushed his dick back inside his pants, zipped it up and went on a verbal rampage.

"I took you out to dinner, bought you drinks, and spent quality time with you. Isn't that what you're always whining about, us spending time together? And now your ungrateful ass can't show gratitude in a way that satisfies me?"

"Dinner, footsie, and boozing don't entitle you to demand sex from me. I'm not your property!" I yelled right back, pulling my dress down and backing away from him.

"The fuck it doesn't. I've got needs too, and you're supposed to be my woman!" Andy said before trying to grab me again.

"Don't touch me!" I screamed, then ran and locked myself in the guestroom.

"Open this door Simone!" Andy demanded as he pounded on the door.

"No. I'm not coming out until you leave."

"Fine. I'll get comfortable on the couch and wait."

I sat on the floor with my back firmly wedged against the door until I heard the *Sports Center Live* theme song blasting from the television. I crept into the living room and stood behind the sofa where Andy sat in the soft spot he made for himself, watching sports highlights. He was seemingly calm, still drunk but calm when I spoke to him.

"Andy, I don't feel safe with you here. Please leave before I call the police."

He jumped up and got in my face. "If you want me to leave, then you're gonna have to throw me out."

"Get out of my house *now!*" I shouted with base in my voice, then walked to the door and yanked it open with so much force the doorknob dented the wall.

"Make me." Andy challenged, getting in my face again.

I shocked myself and shoved his drunken ass so hard he stumbled out the door, and nearly fell to the ground.

He regained his footing then turned and lunged at me. "Why, you fucking bi—"

Before he could finish slurring degrading words, I slammed and locked the door.

He pounded and pounded, "Simone open this door!"

"I'll open it when the police get here."

"Go ahead. Call the police. I hope they drive you to the airport tomorrow." He then paused and said, "What are you two looking at?"

I hurried to the window and pulled back the curtains to find Ritchie and Miss Bonita standing in their doorways watching the circus unfold. Meanwhile, Andy staggered to his car.

"Mr. Man, you shouldn't drive drunk. I can give you a ride. " Ritchie called out.

Andy grabbed his crotch, "Yeah, and I bet your sweet ass wants to ride this, too."

"I don't do tired clowns. I was only offering to get you far away from here in one piece. Good luck getting home dumb-ass." Ritchie said closing his door as I opened mine.

"Young man, I am one digit away from calling the police. Now leave that young lady alone if she doesn't want your company. Get on your way." Miss Bonita warned holding up her phone.

"Andy flailed his hand in Miss Bonita's direction, "Yeah, yeah, yeah. I'll be long gone before they get here."

When he got in his car and drove off I gave Miss Bonita a look of silent thanks. She shook her head as if I was a lost cause then closed her door. I felt like a lost cause as I went back inside, locked and dead bolted my door then wearily went upstairs.

That night, I fell to my knees and prayed for direction, and sanity. But I slept with a box cutter under my pillow just in case Jack Daniels started ruling Andy's mind again.

4

MY LADY

Preoccupation with Traci's wedding set in. Playing the role of bridesmaid had become a personal liability since I wasn't earning big bucks like I used to in Corporate America. But I had to choose to be a bridesmaid to my college roommate and dear friend Traci or my buddy Renee, whose weddings were a week apart. I chose Traci because she was consistently loyal and trustworthy.

Renee was a good friend but her maid-of-honor, Mya Munroe, was attention seeking and notorious for causing trouble. We were all friends since grammar school. But shallow Mya liked to spark petty arguments then fuel them to full-blown fires that surprisingly spilled into my workplace.

One afternoon as I was preparing to go to lunch, Mr. Feinberg, the securities compliance manager, summoned me into his office. His quiet demeanor led me to think hard about what I could have possibly done wrong to warrant an impromptu meeting. *Did I misquote a stock price to a client or sell the wrong asset, or unknowingly violate federal securities laws and rules?*

Mr. Fienberg quickly put my confusion to rest when he pointed to a small stack of papers on the desk bearing familiar handwriting.

"Simone, I am trying to understand why someone named Mya Munroe," he said picking up the cover page and handing it to me, "would jeopardize your job by faxing a ten-page grievance to your workplace about your refusal to participate in someone named Renee's wedding."

I must have turned every shade of red on the color spectrum. I was furious and humiliated at the same time and wanted to fly out of that office and hunt Mya down and beat some sense into her messy behind.

"Mr. Feinberg," I said nervously. "I can't explain why she would do such a thing but I assure you it won't happen again." I placed the page back on the small pile. Mr. Feinberg slid the papers to me.

"They're yours to keep just in case you need them for evidence."

"I don't know what to say."

"You don't have to explain to me. You are one of our most reliable and diligent employees and I don't want your personal life to interfere with your work ethic. Our fax machines are for company business. It's important to inform your um, *friend*, that it is inappropriate and unacceptable to send personal correspondence to your place of work. That's all I want to say about the matter."

"Mr. Feinberg, I appreciate your candor. If it's okay with you, I'd like to go to lunch now and take care of this matter."

"I think that's a good idea. I'll let your supervisor know. And don't worry, your reputation hasn't been tarnished."

"That's reassuring. Thank you, Mr. Feinberg."

Ten minutes later, I ran out of the office to the first pay-phone that I could find to call Mya and tell her ass off while she was still on the clock to get my point across about the separation of work and friendship. I lit into her as soon as I heard her voice on the line.

"Mya how dare you embarrass me at my job acting like you financed my bridesmaid role and couldn't get a refund!"

"Simone, I'm at work. This is not the time to discuss this."

"Listen to me you crazy broad. You fax ten pages of bullshit to my job and then expect me to take your workplace into consideration? I always knew you were self-centered, but this deranged stunt gives you the grand prize for insane!"

"Simone, can we talk about this later?"

"Mya I'm gonna say what I need to say now. If you ever, and I mean *ever* pull that crap again I will kick your messy ass! Do you understand?"

"Simone, if you would listen to what I have to say you'd understand..."

"No, Mya! The only thing I want *you* to understand is don't fuck with my food, my house, my car, in other words, don't ever put me in the position of answering to my job about personal matters that could get me fired. You know my contact numbers. You know where I live. I don't know what possessed you to fax your issue to my job but—"

"Simone please, I can't talk right now."

"Mya there's no more talking. I am through with you. And that means washing and drying my hands of you for good!" I then hung up on her.

After that demoralizing experience, choosing to decline Renee's invitation, was a wise decision, because one catty comment from Mya, about *anything*, my gown, earrings *and* heels were gonna come off and so would Mya's tacky Remy weave once I got my hands in it.

Childish behavior during a major milestone for Renee would have been rude, to say the least. So, I graciously and respectfully declined her bridesmaid invitation.

I then looked forward to seeing Traci walk down the aisle wearing a white princess gown, to marry Brent, the man she called her new best friend. Also, the wedding presented an opportunity to reunite with my stepsisters Shelly, April, and Candace who I hadn't seen in almost twenty years. Traci had unexpected cancellations and suggested that I invite them to make up for her loss.

Our reunion was a long time in the coming. We had a lot of catching up to do and had little time to bond. So Andy not joining me wasn't so tragic after all. Truth be told, his presence would be a burden and without him around I'd have more of a chance for fun in the sand with a Mandingo Warrior.

Frankly, I had grown tired of our topsy-turvy relationship. One minute we were on. The next we were off. One minute Andy was in lust. The next I was threatening to call the police. The wear and tear his dick was putting on Lady—a nickname for my vagina—was wearing me out physically and mentally. After I satisfied his sexual appetite, I was always left hungry for affection. His sex drive was too strong for someone whose performance was lackluster at best in the bedroom.

I'd decided that when I got back from Florida, Andy and I would have our long overdue where-is-this-relationship-going talk.

5

INDEPENDENT WOMAN

A chance meeting almost four years ago brought Andy and me together. Walter, a mutual friend invited us to his twenty-fifth birthday celebration. I arrived fashionably dressed in a slinky black dress, matching pumps, hooker red lipstick, and my signature thong.

DJ Money, a white chocolate, Shemar Moore-type was spinning records, and giving shout-outs.

I had a special request. "Hey DJ, can you play the 'Thong Song" by Sisquo?"

Giving me the once over, he said, "Damn, sexy, I'll play whatever you're wearing under that dress. I bet you're wearing it well, too. Hang out for a minute and talk to me. Can a gentleman get a name?"

"Sure handsome," I answered. "I'm Simone. And you are?"

"Andy, but tonight call me DJ Money. You married?"

"Negative."

"Dating?"

"Nope."

"Looking."

"No, but I like what I see," I flirted.

"That doesn't answer my question."

"I like what I'm looking at. How about you. Kids? Dating? Girlfriend? Wife?"

"No across the board. You got kids?"

"No. I'm an independent woman with a clean bill of health." I said inching up my dress thigh-high. Before I could expose my satin thong, Walter entered the room, bringing an abrupt end to my shameless flirting.

Walter had been trying to get close to me for a while, but I was against sleeping with a friend, since that rarely ended well.

Still, Walter tried everything in his power to keep Andy and me from hooking up. He pretended to "lose" my telephone number, and once he told Andy that I'd moved out of town, and funniest of all, that I was married.

But Andy was a smooth talker on a mission who wouldn't be denied. He probed Walter for more details and even demanded my number.

Walter warned him, "Nah, man. You don't want to mess with Simone. She's about business. Your player shit ain't gonna work on her."

"Dude, stop cock blocking and give me her number and throw in her address." Andy demanded, ignoring Walter's not so subtle warning.

"Do you want a road map, too?" Walter half-joked.

"How much is all of this gonna cost me?" Andy went as far as offering monetary consideration for my deets but Walter couldn't be bought.

"Nah, I can't put a price on Simone's privacy. Keep your money. You ain't ready for her. Trust me. She's not the wild, loose woman you're used to dealing with on the club scene. Simone doesn't need your smooth talk, pennies and lies. She's too good of a woman for the game. You'll just have to pray on seeing her again."

Walter withheld my contact information, serious about protecting his someone special he would never have.

Nearly three years went by before I crossed paths with Andy on a midnight boat cruise where lust finally prevailed. I was even more attracted to his good looks, and six-foot plus frame. I never thought to question his character. At that time, his integrity was a non-factor for me. I was horny as hell.

On the upper deck I watched the crowd dance to hip-hop, reggae, R&B, and house music. I journeyed from the deck to the dance floor. On the way a man looking every bit of a cup of mocha almond coffee asked me to dance. Working the swing of my hips to the sexy tune of "Too Close", I caught the attention of Andy and his buddies. I was relentless in my pursuit and feeling myself as my dance partner's member bulged in the seat of his pants. I was turned off by him, but turned on watching Andy as I danced.

When the song changed to a slow track I sat on a bench in direct view of Andy. I wanted him to see me, all of me, every inch and every curve.

Andy was looking fine standing on the sideline, contemplating when to stick his hook in my mouth for the reel in. Little did he know, I was ready and available for the snatch— hook, line, and sinker. I zoomed in on his rod to see what he was packing for bait. His crotch didn't reveal much of a bulge, but I was on a mission to inspect, touch and feel his total package. Until that happened, I blew sensual kisses his way.

The vibe was right, in no time Andy caved to the allure of my sex appeal. He was so enthralled by my presence, he found himself walking in my direction led by his ego. A man being a man, Andy had to prove to his buddies that he knew me, the curvaceous honey in the black spandex pants, sheer silver blouse and three-inch leather pumps. Radar was locked. I was the target. For me, the timing couldn't have been better. I was fresh over a seven-year relationship with my ex-boyfriend Clay Marshall. Scars had healed, but emotional wounds still ran deep. I was ready to forget about him.

Andy must've been telepathic because he cut straight to his chase and put his rap on as thick as the night was humid.

"It's been too long, but worth the wait. Take down my number and give me yours."

"Wait. Who said I was available?"

"You. The way you're dressed, it's in your eyes, and all those air kisses you've been blowing."

"Fair enough. I'm single, but not desperate."

"I didn't say anything about desperate, but I will say you are just as sexy as you were when I first met you."

"Oh you mean when we met at Walter's—"

"We're not talking about Walter tonight. When can I see you again and I don't want to wait another three years for an answer."

"Tonight, after the boat docks."

"Oh, I see you waste no time going after what you want."

"Well, you know what they say about time, we only have it to waste and it never comes back. It's tonight or never."

"Sexy, sophisticated, straightforward, and self-confident." Andy smiled at me.

"So you approve?" I asked coyly.

"Indeed I do."

The conquest was no obstacle. It wasn't necessary for Andy to bore me with small talk. I had already decided that he would be my man and I would be his woman. After the boat cruise encounter, we started what I thought would be a romantic relationship flooded with intense excitement, love, and happiness, as we committed ourselves to each other for life.

Andy didn't have a whole lot of money to speak of, but he was making top dollar as a master plumber, and producing mixed tapes on the side. His cash flow may not have been in abundance but he was still earning enough money to pay his rent. And since he wasn't living out of garbage bags and sleeping on somebody's couch, it confirmed his commitment to make ends meet by any legal means necessary. Andy was his own man. I really had no reason to suspect him of anything shady.

After spending weeks sharing details of our life, dining out, and occasional walks around Charles River, we became an item. The deal was sealed. I was his and he was mine.

Early in our relationship, Andy seduced me with kindness and won me over with generosity. He was liberal with his time, showed off his plumbing skills on small jobs around my house, and wined and dined me without expecting anything in return. A day never came and went when he didn't call on his lunch hour to whisper sweet, sexy things in my ear; every breathy word traveled straight between my legs. The mere sound of his charming voice overwhelmed me and filled Lady with pulsating ecstasy.

Eight months later, sex fiend Andy surfaced. Things weren't the same between us once he started constantly nagging me for sex, and trying to take it whenever he wanted it. The honeymoon was clearly over.

A peculiar darkness shrouded Andy's good looks. He'd changed from the Andy I had met almost four years ago at Walter's birthday party. That Andy was brassier, and rougher around the edges. He was extremely cocky, and I liked the bad boy vibe about him.

The new Andy, as I had come to know him was no longer driving me around in a sports car the color of money. A dusty gray Cougar that rattled when he tried to showoff and push the odometer over thirty had replaced it. Andy's material possessions weren't the only things to have escaped him, so had his compassion and care. Andy stopped doing small jobs around the house. His once attentive, supportive, and fun disposition grew cold, and confusing; as did his unreasonable sexual expectations.

Charming me for sex was the only thing Andy seemed to make time for. If he had his way, he would have helped himself to the "sexy pussy" between my legs every chance he could. But I was finished with selfish Andy. His chances of sleeping with me in the future became as good as Walter's—nil.

6

DIRTY TALK

Deeper into our relationship, drama continued to unfold as Andy transformed into "a double- minded man. He was Doctor Evil and Mister Fickle, rolled into one. His mood changed with the time of day. Andy could not make up his mind about anything, in particular our bipolar relationship. One week we were an item, the next we were back to being "just friends." I went out of my way to remind Andy that friends don't sleep with friends. As usual, those words were ignored. He tried taking sex from me when he wanted it.

When his behavior and attitude changed for the worse, his generosity and kindness disappeared like a bar of cheap soap. Distance was between us. We stopped playing Mancala, Scrabble, and Backgammon. He didn't tickle me the way he used to. Gone were the nights when I was paralyzed by laughter, too weak to break the grip of his masculine arms. He would start by cornering me on the couch, or wherever he found me relaxing, and then we would hit the floor before the night was over. That's the Andy I missed: passionate Andy, his jokes and laughter, and even the torture of his tickle.

But board games became head games, laughter turned into tears, and closeness was replaced by tension. My Daddy would roll over and kick dirt off his grave if he knew I had taken up with a brazen wolf disguised as my sheep, too far removed from his emotions to love me back.

As time went on, I changed in the love game, too. Andy's agenda became mine: sex, sex, sex, and more sex. I actually got off on the sound of him whimpering into total submission at Lady's prowess. Lady helped weaken the grip he had on my emotions. He was under her spell and powerless. He was no match for me in the bedroom. Andy was like putty in my hands. After every body slapping session, Andy would ask, "Is my dick as good to you as your pussy is to me?"

I couldn't answer the question with a straight face, so I'd just nod.

"Show me." Andy would say.

I'd smile and turn my attention to his stiff inviting penis. Then, I hypnotized him with dirty talk, as I'd hover my lips over his dick. The tease was on in front of a floor mirror.

"How deep in my mouth do you want me to take it?"

"Take it as far as you want, just don't bite it off."

Before I went down south, I let Andy kiss me softly all over my silky smooth body. He was sweating out of his skin, begging me to go deep. "Suck it now. Suck it now. I'm about to explode!" He shouted for pleasure.

"All over me?" I asked. By then, Andy was drooling.

"Woman, where did you come from? I'm about to bust a walnut!"

"Hang on. Let me show you where I came from. Now say pretty please," I purred.

"Pretty Woman! Ugly Betty! Beautiful Liar! Sexy Simone! Suck it now damn it!" Andy shouted.

On command, I slipped his dick in my mouth as far back as it would go and then sucked with the intensity of a vacuum cleaner.

The grip of my lips and the motion of my tongue operated with slutty authority. Andy moaned and groaned in blissful agony. His toes were scrunched tight. His fists were clenched even tighter.

Andy pulled my hair, and yanked my head back until my mouth opened wide.

"Let me come inside you." He begged, clutching and massaging his penis.

"No. I'm not on birth control so for now put it all right here." I spread my legs, and cupped my hands in front of Lady. In a matter of seconds, Andy's sperm covered my palms.

Minutes later, Andy was snoring a whipped man's melody. I retired to the couch knowing that lust did not make a relationship and that Andy would disappointment me if I didn't get off our relationship rollercoaster ride sooner rather than later.

Dozing off, my mother's wisdom came to mind. *Simone, lust can keep a relationship together, but denial will break your heart.*

7

"STRUNG OUT"

P acked and ready to go, my one and only travel bag sat at the front door as I waited for my sister Susan to drive me to the train station. I didn't expect Andy to show up after I threatened to call the police on him last night.

I gave Susan specific instructions to arrive a quarter to the hour, and I prayed, "Lord, please give Susan the will to be patient. Please don't let her honk the horn, or yell my name out, announcing my departure to the busy bodies of Peyton Place." The moment I said, "Amen", music about people having to have money blasted from Susan's car speakers on the other side of my window.

I remembered the O'Jays hit song, "Money, Money, Money", being played during block parties when all was safe in the neighborhood. There were no stray bullets and no crack co-caine, just street partying until the early morning, or until the cops shut us down. Safe partying and dancing in the streets was had long before chemical warfare and black market guns threatened to destroy the core of the community with self-destruction and senseless violence.

As drug dealing, substance abuse and addiction infiltrated our neighborhoods, the sounds of guns discharging, and sirens wailing became commonplace. Innocent bystanders and young soldiers died premature deaths by way of homicide, often times the result of illegal guns that fell into the wrong hands. Bodies riddled with bullet holes were discarded in the gutter. Families were left with grief and the unbearable task of burying their children years "before their time".

The community was in a state of crisis. Drug lords, pushers, and an emergence of Youth gangs ruled the streets. Female addicts scuffed their precious knees paying homage to their pusher's dick. The word was out: one hit and you were hooked on a high so high it would make a woman sell her baby, her food stamps and her jewels, all for a drag on a crack pipe.

It was one big ugly mess. "Down with dope, up with hope", was empty rhetoric. So I emptied my bank account and fled south on my academic journey.

Susan wasn't spared from drug addiction. She was born four years and one month before Mother pushed me out. When Mother went to work, Susan wore the pants. Daddy wasn't around. Mother left his abusive ways before I turned six.

Growing up, Susan was witty. She always had interesting things to say. Her personality was larger-than-life. She had maternal instincts that transferred to her own three children. She spent many nights reading Monica, Sasha and Dallas bedtime stories and planning birthday parties one year in advance. But drugs nearly ruined Susan. She turned her back on her children, and left them without shoes on their feet to chase a chemical high in the streets. When Susan's leaf fell from the family tree, she became the family's black sheep.

It was a crying shame when Family Services filed a 51 A for reckless and cruel abandonment. But they were my family and it was my responsibility to take them in and offer a sense of stability.

My worse recollection of Susan being "hooked" brought to mind the image of her strung out, skeletal frame strolling Blue Hill Ave. One hot summer night, she went car to car wearing only a flimsy dress, begging for money, and most likely offering her body in return for a quick fix. I was next. Susan knocked on the front passenger window, grinning a toothless grin. She didn't even know who I was, but I recognized her and her sad state shamed me. I sadly chose not to acknowledge her. In fact, I didn't even make eye contact. On that night, I disowned strung out Susan as my sister. When the light turned green, I stepped on the accelerator and left a trail of smoke that hid her from my view.

Luke 6:37: *Do not judge and you will not be judged . . .Forgive and you will be forgiven,* helped me excuse Susan for her past indiscretions. I forgave her, letting bygones be bygones. Susan was no longer addicted and that's all that mattered to me. I continued to pray that she would stay clean for her children's sake, and my sanity.

8

THE BIGGER THE WALLET

The telephone rang as I prepared to roll my luggage out the door. I thought twice about answering it knowing that needy friends dialed my line off the hook when their self-esteem was so low their reflection seemed invisible in the mirror to them.

Values of friendship, however I can define them, led me to the receiver.

"Hello. State your problem." I said with my usual Miller attitude.

"Simone, I'm glad you're home. I need to talk."

Keisha's voice was filled with worry. I suspected her married lover had finally left her for his wife.

Keisha Bailey and I met ten years ago while working part time at a local bookstore. She was a junior at the Art Institute while I worked hard to get through my sophomore year at Business University.

In retrospect, I have to assume responsibility for the slowing of my progress wheel. In those days, I had some misplaced priorities of my own. I was a slave to a paycheck, a shop-a-holic, and head-over-hills-in-love with my boyfriend at the time, Clay. I was living life to the hilt. I had my own home, and supported myself financially on a comfortable income. In my spare time, I found my craft in styling hair, something I've been doing since I was yay-big. I practiced for years on my best friend Cindy. She was my Guinea pig. From the first plat, to rows of cornbraids, Cindy was a model student.

The greatest satisfaction came when satisfied customers paid with cash. Credit wasn't accepted. If they showed up without money they had to reschedule when they got their funds right.

At the tender age of twenty-something my corporate earnings and hair styling revenue amassed a down payment on a single-family Colonial, across from the biggest Cathedral on my side of town.

Keisha pulled me from my thoughts.

"Simone, are you still there? It's Keisha."

"I know it's you calling because your wallet-chasing aura reeks of more married-man problems."

"And that means what?"

"It means, the bigger the wallet, the quicker you lower your guard and find yourself in trouble and calling me for advice again."

"That's not true."

"Damn right it is. You complain my ear off knowing that you're not going to take the advice you ask for. Then I won't hear from you until the next flair-up. So, let's hear it. What's your issue today? And speed up the tape, I don't have all morning to talk."

"Well, excuse me. It's not like you've got a job to go to."

"Listen smart alec, I'm on my way to Florida."

"Okay. I only need a few minutes to talk about something serious."

"Does this something serious have to do with the married man that almost got you locked up for calling his wife?"

"Simone, he's not just married, he's a big spender. Right now I'm wearing a snazzy pair of Jimmy Choo pumps. They were delivered to my job with a note asking me to meet him at the Millennium so he can apologize."

"Are you going?"

"Of course, and I'll be wearing these pumps and a trench coat with very little on underneath."

"Keisha I think you're wasting your time, but that's my opinion."

"As long as he gives me money and spoils me with gifts, I'm gonna be his good-time-girl."

"You might be a good-time-girl to him, but you're only a distraction from his problems at home. At some point your heart is going to demand more and he won't give it to you because it belongs to someone else."

"Who said I was after his heart?"

"So throwing a pair of shoes at your feet and slipping a few dollars in your pockets is enough to make you content with being his call girl?"

"Freak you, you self-righteous snob."

"You know I couldn't resist that dig since you seem to think him giving you material gifts makes him an honest man."

"Simone, you're so smug about everything. That shit really irks me. You're my girl, but please mess up soon so I can wash your face in your mistakes."

"Ouch. Don't get so touchy. I'm just trying to calm my nerves before I get on the plane."

"Anyway, Gordon is pressuring me to have unprotected sex."

"Keisha be safe with your body. Please use condoms at all times. No exceptions. And I'm not saying this because I condone your affair, I'm saying it as a friend who cares and wants you to make healthy decisions. Don't go stupid for shoes and money. Neither is worth risking your health so he can get his dick wet."

"Simone I'm not gonna lie sometimes I want that skin-to-skin experience, not to mention put it on his ass so good he'd write me in his will."

"You're delusional if you think he'd think about you on that level of importance to him. I've gotta go. Susan is waiting to give me a ride to the train station. Let me get going before she loses patience and starts honking like a maniac."

"Why is Susan giving you a ride? Where's Andy? Are you two fighting again?"

"He's at work and none of your business. Now can we talk when I get back?"

"Simone, you're telling me that I have to wait until you return to figure out a solution? How can you leave me in this dilemma? I need your help. What should I do? Condom on or condom off?"

"You're kidding, right?"

"No. I'm serious. Should I fuck his rich ass raw or not?"

"Keisha don't let his married dick spark a fire in your pussy that water can't put out. Does that answer your question?"

"You are too much." Keisha laughed off her embarrassment. "Girl, go and have fun for me, too. We can catch up when you get back. By then I should have this dilemma figured out."

"Dilemma?" It was Simone's turn to laugh. "What is there to figure out? I think you've been playing that married man's fool long enough."

"Like I said, mess up soon. I can't wait!"

"If and when I do, you won't know about it. And don't hate me for being honest. Just wish me a safe trip and we'll rap when I return. Oh, before we hang up let me give you a final word of advice."

"Yeah, and what's that?" Keisha asked as though she couldn't care less about my opinion. I voiced it anyway.

"Think about giving your pussy a break. Put a clamp on it. You don't want her shriveled up like a prune. No decent man will marry damaged goods, with married men miles on it."

"Witch, you know what . . ."

I stopped Keisha in mid sentence before she could tell me off.

"I don't want to hear it. Seriously, this witch has gotta go."

Keisha laughed. "Fly nice and don't forget your 'mad money'."

I laughed with her, "I don't need it; Andy isn't joining me."

Rubbing my temples I was relieved to finally hang up because Keisha's dilemma stressed my brain and made my hangover worse.

Rushing to leave the house, I prayed silently, *let the wise listen and add to their learning, and let the discerning get guidance . . .* "And that goes for me, too." I added.

9

BE ANXIOUS FOR NOTHING

Susan started honking just as I opened my door. I sucked my teeth knowing I should have been waiting on the sidewalk because patience has never been her virtue.

"My bell works!" I shouted over the noise to avoid a circus scene.

Susan rolled down her window. "Would you hurry up so we can go; it's eight forty five. I've got to take Sasha to camp and make it to my chiropractor appointment before nine thirty."

When Susan said, "chiropractor", I knew she was in a hurry because she believed in capitalizing on car accidents even if she was at fault. I grabbed my bag and hurried out the door forgetting to set the house alarm. At that moment, I didn't care who had what appointment and making it to my destination became secondary knowing that locked doors, and the Neighborhood Watch still didn't deter thieves. I had too much to lose. I stole another minute of Susan's time to set the alarm.

After securing the house, I got in the passenger seat and waved to Sasha who was sitting in the back. The ride to the train station was uneventful, apart from Susan's lead foot. I had to remind her time after time to slow down. My nagging didn't stop her road rage. Money was on her mind and safety didn't matter. All I could do was shake my head in disgust while thinking, *Andy, Keisha, and Susan in a span of two days, was a bit much. I* popped two aspirins and washed them down with spring water. Sasha sat quietly in the back seat, completely out of character. Usually, she's the life of the car. Sasha, Susan's middle child, was by far the wisest, compared to her thinks-she's-grown sister Monica and her rambunctious brother Dallas. I was disappointed that I didn't get to answer Sasha's usual twenty questions. I was ready whenever she was, but the questions never came. Susan got me to Forest Hills Train Station in five minutes flat. Ten would've been normal.

At curbside, Susan and I exchanged sisterly hugs and said our good-byes because traveling was too great of a risk to part ways on bad terms. I hugged Sasha and asked her to look out for her brother Dallas and sister Monica.

Softly she said, "Roger that," and gave me the thumbs up.

Off I went to board the waiting train bound for Logan Airport.

I arrived at the departure gate thirty minutes before takeoff appropriately dressed for my trip south wearing cotton shorts, a one-size-too-small tee shirt to accentuate my firm tits, a jean jacket and comfy sneakers. I made my way to the souvenir shop to take my mind off flying, which never excited me, although it was supposed to be the safest means of transportation—compared to the alternatives. Flying the friendly skies takes the least amount of time, with a relatively low chance of fatalities, unless of course, suicide extremists hijacked the plane. In that event, at least I could justify my last gripe over lousy airline food.

The final boarding announcement came over the PA. I took my carry-on bag, souvenirs, and headed for the gate. Without further delay, my row was called. I boarded the plane, found my way to coach, and took the aisle seat. Several minutes later we were airborne.

Flight attendants followed routine and demonstrated the "dos" and "don'ts", and proper conduct while in the air, ordering us to stay seated with electronic devices in the off position. A deep-throated, masculine voice boomed from the PA speaker directly above my head, welcoming crewmembers and passengers onboard; I secretly prayed it was the captain and not a hijacker. After the announcement, I relaxed my body, tightened the straps on the seat belt, and waited for permission to move about the cabin.

"You are now free to move about the cabin," was announced minutes later. I had nowhere to go, but was at liberty to wander. I unfastened the seatbelt, and reclined the chair back as far as it would go. I didn't see any germs but I knew they were in the air. I tried my best not to inhale too deeply. The air conditioner was on full blast. The cabin was ice-cold. The chill didn't seem to bother my fellow Caucasian passengers seeing that skiing was their favorite sport because that's all they talked about since they sat down. "Their flight to Colorado must have been canceled," I told myself although I wanted them to shut up so I could envision sunshine and palm trees instead of mountains and snow. They continued to carry on. I pushed the call-button for the flight attendant. She answered immediately, greeting me with a friendly sky smile.

"Yes. May I help you?"

"I hope so. It's quite cold. May I have a pillow, a blanket, and ear plugs?"

"Sorry Miss, but we're out of pillows and blankets. The airline doesn't supply ear plugs."

"Thanks anyway." I sat back and sighed . . . "It's going to be a long ride south."

Four hours later and twelve minutes behind schedule, the plane was safely on the ground in Tampa, Florida. All the credit went to God even though I thought I was going to catch pneumonia and ruin my trip.

Eager to deplane, I grabbed my carry-on bag, and rushed off as if the love of my life was waiting for me at the altar. Then I had to remind myself, "Be anxious for nothing."

10

THE GOLDEN RULE

Tradition called for Brent to propose to Traci. He kneeled on both knees, and she was ecstatic to say yes. For Traci, marriage meant an end to dating setbacks and the beginning of endless love. I was happy and sad for Traci. Happy because she deserved the best and kept her faith, sad because I would be losing another friend. First my best friend Cindy relocated out of Boston, and then my dear friend Traci was ready to say "I do."

The holy sacrament of marriage is a blessing and a serious commitment. I didn't despair because Andy was half way *in* my life, which made me only half lonely. Strange, though, when he wasn't around I only felt alone.

"Room Dunes for Life" was a pact Traci and I made freshmen year at Fairmont University, during our good ole days of midnight sex romps with Kappa fraternity brothers.

The parties! The frat boys! What more could two horny girls have asked for? We boozed it up until the wee hours of the morning, slipping and sliding on the diving board, and enjoying multiple orgasms in T. Brown Park after dark. We were sex criminals who could effortlessly seduced frat boys out of their krimson and kreme boxers. Traci and I fucked and sucked them until they crowned us in-the-heat-of-the-moment-honorary-Kappa sweethearts.

I was the humble one and Traci had an aura about her that represented an affluent Black family, a status symbol on a predominantly Historical Black College campus. But a silver spoon didn't exempt Traci from heartache. She had her fair share of rickety emotional roller-coaster rides to prove her pain, too.

Traci was a hot commodity for the Kappa Casanovas, the real pretty ones. At times, she would compromise her values and lower her self-worth to one-night stands with creeps whose screw 'em and leave 'em attitude showed Traci that she was only good for her platinum credit cards.

But my How To Get Laid for Dummies 101 intervention always put Traci back in control of their minds and their campus dicks.

The Golden Rule: If you want him to want you, don't make his conquest too easy. Traci learned early on to pussy-whip the sponges before they got too deep into her heart. She was a quick learner. In a short time, the Krimson and Kreme players got what they wanted — casual sex and merciless blowjobs. But they didn't conquer Traci's emotions. Instead, they were left begging for more.

My best recollection of teaching Traci how to win in the lust game was the night of the Kappa's annual luau-themed Fresh Meat party.

"Look at him. Doesn't he look scrumptious?" I asked Traci standing next to me in the dark frat house where we and the other homesick kittens were on the menu. A tall frat brother, looking long in the pants, started walking toward me. Tugging on my hula skirt, I got nervous and insecure, and it showed in my face. I didn't know if I was gonna succeed or fail at showing Traci how to use charisma and sex appeal to seduce his mind before he could start running his fraternity player game on me. But I was prepared to give her a memorable lesson.

Finally, face-to-face he looked like Blair Underwood's twin and he smelled of spicy cologne. The masculine scent made Lady purr.

"I'm sorry, I didn't catch your name." Fraternity guy said suavely.

"That's because I haven't thrown it your way yet. " I answered, gently biting my lower lip in what I hoped was a teasing manner.

Traci whispered in my ear, "You've got it going on. I didn't know you handled them smooth like that. I just might learn something tonight. Teach on."

I was encouraged.

He smiled. "I'm Ralph, sexy. I can tell I'm going to keep you around for a long time." Fraternity guy said pretty sure of himself.

My devilish gaze met his hungry stare, and then trailed down his face, his chest, finally stopping at his crotch before I said, "Simone. Pleased to make your acquaintance."

He smiled wider, and then asked, "Are you good with numbers because I've got seven to lay on you."

Flirting right back, I said, "My memory bank is all yours, feed me."

At that moment, Ralph removed a Hawaiian lei from his neck and wrapped it around mine, signaling to the frat that I was marked territory.

Traci made her exit. "Nice work. I'll be around," she whispered.

"Check in with me before you leave, especially if you're not leaving alone" I told her and then winked.

Hours later leading into dawn, Ralph's mouth desired and practically devoured every inch of me. If he had any thoughts of pumping and dumping me, I could sense by the love his lips, teeth and tongue were making to my body, his dick didn't have a choice but to want me around for a long time, even if it meant Ralph making me his undercover campus fuck. Before the sun could say good morning, I was officially initiated in Ralph's frat house bed, where he begged me to stay for the night, and the next night.

Three weeks into our sexual trysts, Ralph evolved from sensual to trifling after I learned he was working my dorm, Ruby Hall right under my nose. Talk of his philandering surfaced one morning in the campus-dining hall where I sat with dorm mates being schooled on who to screw and who to snub. I was caught off guard when a sophomore name Leah started whining about Ralph stepping out on her, creeping around campus after midnight picking up and dropping off his secret lover, yours truly. She claimed to have found used condoms in his trashcan to prove she wasn't the only one he was humping. When someone said, "At least he's using protection."

Leah replied, "Yeah, with them, but not with me."

Butterflies swarmed my stomach. I was on the verge of an anxiety attack knowing that every time Ralph and I had sex, I would start with tongue teasing the tip of his penis, then licking the shaft and blowing air on his balls before sucking him down my throat. The thought of Leah's body fluids made me want to puke. I stood up so quickly that I bumped the table and a glass of orange juice spilled into her lap. Leah gave me a death stare and shook her head. "Clumsy much", she said, wiping up the juice.

"I'm sorry. I'm sorry." I apologized and then took off running like a misfit from the dining hall. I crossed the busy street heading for the dorm, and didn't bother looking in both directions. When I reached Ruby Hall, I ran up the stairs to my room and threw myself on my bed and sobbed my hurt out. I felt betrayed, used and foolish, and vowed to get revenge on Ralph's campus dick. One day came and went before vengeance was mine. The first strike against Ralph was a vile message left on his answering machine.

"Campus creep of the night, I want to know why you're sticking your dick in another pussy without protection. You better pray my STD test is negative otherwise you're gonna be sorry you asked me my name."

Ralph phoned later begging me to listen to his side of the story, which turned into a lame excuse about the pressures of being a fraternity man.

"Simone, you know how it is around campus. The girls flock to us frat guys. Sometimes I feel like I have to grow another dick, one especially for you, and another casual one for them."

"Are you serious?"

Ralph laughed, "Of course not. I just wanted to explain how hard it is to resist temptation. Are you coming over so I can say sorry with a massage, foot rub, and—"

"Hell no! Now I know why a dog is a man's best friend. Bye!"

I dropped Ralph quicker than a Physics class, got myself tested for venereal diseases, passed them all, and moved on to a kinder, gentler, Kappa. His line name was, "Trojan Man."

Memories of risqué college days faded. My mind switched to being a bridesmaid and how much I adored Traci and our stable sister-friendship. All these years later, I realized that we have come too far to grow old apart.

I could only recall one time Traci came close to a breach of trust. One day, she schemed to destroy my Whitney Houston cassette while I was away at class. Listening to Whitney's music on constant repeat was an essential part of my daily ritual. From sun-up, in between classes, to dusk, "Where Do Broken Hearts Go", soared from my boom box. The sad lyrics expressed how I felt—like a lovesick fool addicted to somber music, and I didn't even have a boyfriend to pine over. Traci felt sorry for me so she didn't destroy my cassette.

Before arriving in Florida, I warned Traci not to be surprised that I chopped off my hair for a crop cut. I purposely didn't mention the few extra pounds I gained since we last saw each other a couple years ago. Last weigh-in, I tipped the scale at about 135, twenty pounds heavier than I was fifteen years ago. But I still looked good and loved my curves.

When Traci and I connected in Tampa International Airport, she welcomed me with a sincere smile and a warm hug. She then stepped back to look me over.

"Simone, you look great and I love your new hairdo. I see you've picked up some weight in all the right places." Traci turned me around to examine my assets. "Hmm. I bet Andy's been busy working that sexy body overtime."

I chuckled at the notion of Andy putting-it-on-*me* in the bedroom. Self-conscious about my new curves, I didn't tell Traci that double fudge mocha ice cream and pasta deserved full credit for my extra padding.

Our first order of business was to shorten my dress for a polished fit. En route to the dressmaker, Traci gave me a quick run-down of the wedding party's agenda. She talked candidly about how fortunate she was to be marrying Brent. In her heart, he was "the one." She seemed certain of that. He had to be doing something right in between the sheets for my girl to accept him as her life partner. Although, I was surprised when Traci admitted to being nervous about an exclusive relationship. Not remotely engaged, I could relate to her trepidation knowing that sharing closet space and losing solitude was the ultimate sacrifice of an independent woman. For those reasons, I didn't mind bench warming in the dug out, in no hurry to go from unhappily dating, to married and insanely miserable at home plate. Nevertheless, I remained open to the idea of companionship. I assured Traci that she was in good hands with Brent. After all, she was marrying her soul mate.

Continuing with our rounds, we went to Floral Express to purchase table decorations. After that trip, we made an impromptu visit to Traci's parents' house.

Oblivious of our presence, Traci's mom, biological father, and his female-friend were engrossed in deep conversation. I assumed, judging by the wedding paraphernalia scattered about that they were finalizing expenses—a hairy matter, especially when money was being spent on 200 hundred guests—most they might never see or hear from again.

Traci and I made our presence known, and then got comfortable, and barefoot in the dining room where we ate a plate of tuna fish casserole and chased the meal with a tall glass of ice water. I secretly prayed for the meal to hold me over for the rest of the evening, since pounds were easy to come and much harder to lose.

Our bellies were full. Dessert for me was served on a silver platter and presented by Traci. She gave me a plaque inscribed with the sentiment: *Friendship is precious like silver. Once it's tarnished, it never shines the same again. Cherish true friendship.* Overwhelmed by emotions, I was tongue-tied, a state Andy would find hard to believe no matter the circumstances. Still, I managed to express my gratitude with tears in lieu of words. The plaque affirmed my love and respect for our friendship.

After spending quality time with her family, we called it a night, and hit the road.

꧁

"Traci, look out for that car!" I panicked, and then grabbed the steering wheel to veer Traci's Jetta to the side of the road just in time to miss a car coming at us head on. "Good gracious! We almost got crushed! Traci, where on the road were your eyes that you didn't see that car coming? The high beams were blinding. It was impossible to miss *them.* Don't tell me you're bailing out on Brent and trying to check me out with you. What's going on?"

"Simone, chill out. I had it under control, but I was thinking about giving up my freedom to marriage. What are you giving up besides lip tonight?" Traci asked sarcastically, as she pulled back onto the highway.

"I don't believe this. We're actually fighting. Traci pull over."

She kept driving, pushing the odometer pass the legal speed limit.

"Traci. Pull over, now!"

"For what Simone, a frigging lecture about the values of marriage? I'm not in the mood for a speech. Let me deal with this my way."

"Pull this car over now or I will jump in the driver's seat and do it myself."

Traci stopped in the breakdown lane about a quarter mile from the hotel. She turned to me laughing. "You're right. We are fighting."

We got out the car and started screaming, "We're fighting! We're fighting!"

The State Trooper parked in the cut didn't find our actions amusing. We were cited for unlawful use of a breakdown lane and disorderly conduct. He then ordered us back in the car.

On the road again I reached into the ashtray filled with loose change, pulled out a copper coin, holding it up for Traci to see, "Penny for your thoughts."

"There's nothing to share. I think you know the story. A woman approaching her prime gotta do what a woman's gotta do."

"Which is?"

"Get married and start a family."

"Sounds like the dream of every woman over thirty."

"Maybe. But I don't know if I'm completely ready even though Brent is a great guy. He comes from a God-fearing family, he wants to build a future with a house full of kids, and he treats me like a queen. I don't want to walk away from our future because I may never meet a decent man like Brent again." Traci admitted and then broke down crying.

"Let me see. God fearing. Check. Paternal instincts. Check. Makes you feel like a queen. Triple check. Is Brent still employed as an Applications Engineer?" When Traci nodded I continued. "Brent is a good natured, responsible and gainfully employed man who wants to settle down and make a life with you. He would be a stable provider who wants to give you a world of happiness. Why on earth would you think about walking away and possibly ending up with a jerk who isn't fit to be a father, much less husband material? Who can measure up to the unconditional quality of life that Brent can give you and your children?"

"Simone, that's just it. There's no one else. I'm scared we might grow apart. I don't want to get hurt like my mother did when my father fell out of love with her and made her a single parent."

"You're not your mother and Brent is not your father. Marriage is challenging but honest and civil communication can be the secret to avoid divorce. Oh, and keep meddling folks out your business. Fix problems at home, or seek marriage counseling. Now what is your heart telling you to do?"

Traci looked at me and smiled. "It's telling me to marry the man that I love and to have faith in the power of prayer when and if our vows are tested. Thanks for helping me find clarity."

"Any time girlfriend. Remember, let the Lord see you through, unless you want me to slap some sense into your worried head. Just say the word."

"Simone, you're right." Traci agreed drying her tears. "I need to put my worries in God's hands and trust His guidance."

"That's right. Keep the faith. Now let's go to the hotel because I'm exhausted."

"Same here."

Traci and I made the rest of the trip in silence, arriving at the Marriott, where the bridal party was staying, without further incident.

The long day ended with a bubble bath and foot massage, compliments of me.

11

BAD MANNERS

One day down and reuniting with my stepsisters was hours away. Curious about their whereabouts, I telephoned the front desk to inquire if they had checked in. There was no Shelly, April or Candace on the registry. Right away, I thought, *how inconsiderate of them to back out without notice.* But it wasn't like they owed me an explanation. I had no grounds to blame them for not showing up. We didn't have fond memories of growing up as siblings in a loving household. We also hadn't seen each other in over twenty years.

The only memory I would expect them to have of me was a cruel sign language gesture inviting them to kiss my derriere. A blow of a kiss, a pat on the chest, and a slap on my ass, said it all. The southern belles got the message and delivered it straight to Daddy. My, or I should say, *our* Daddy asked me, "Why'd you tell your sisters to kiss your ass?"

"They kept staring at me," I shrugged. "City folk consider staring rude."

"Get your ass back in there and apologize for acting too city in my house! And, leave those bad manners up north where they belong." He ordered.

Daddy was furious. I never saw him that upset before. I didn't talk back to him like I sassed Mother because he didn't take any sass and was always quick with discipline. I did what I was told, and fumed, *Sellouts! Country folks aren't supposed to know city language.* I wanted out and away from Daddy's new family. And to make sure my departure happened sooner rather than as scheduled, I cried every day and every night after the fact. A week later, I was sent home.

Twenty years later, I hoped they wouldn't hold my bad manners against me.

12

THE COMPANY WE KEEP

The official countdown started for Traci to be off the market and starting her life with Brent.

First order of business was picking up my dress from the seamstress. Grabbing a pair of knee-his was a higher priority since I expected my period that weekend.

Brenda, the maid-of -honor, joined Traci and I on the final rounds since she had loose ends of her own to tie up. We picked up my dress, and delivered table decorations to the reception hall where Brenda engaged in small talk with the event coordinators.

After we finished our errands, Traci and I returned to the hotel. I checked the registry again, hoping my stepsisters had arrived, or at least left a message saying they were delayed by traffic. But they hadn't. I didn't get neurotic or throw a hissy fit because my main reason for being in Florida was to escape social drama, relax, and support Traci's wedding, and I was doing just that.

Early that evening, the entire sixteen person bridal party met in the courtyard for a pre-rehearsal dinner meet-and-greet. I finally met Brent and his best man, Steve. Brent had a round face, with playful chubby cheeks, a small potbelly, and a pleasant, nerdy personality. We clicked right away. Brent used our brief introduction to get to know his future wife better through her friend, since in theory, we are only as good as the company we keep.

"Simone, it's an honor to finally meet Traci's closest confidante and friend." Brent greeted me as though he was prepared to interrogate me about Traci's wild college days.

"It's a pleasure to finally meet you as well. I've heard wonderful things about you." I said with a big smile.

"Well, I wish we had time to catch up like we were old friends." Brent chuckled. "I'm sure you have some interesting stories to share."

"Brent, I admire your sense of humor. Traci always loved a good laugh." I deflected his question.

"So you and Traci laughed a lot at Fairmont University?"

"Absolutely. Do you know what she'd find funny today?"

"No." Brent slid in closer to whisper. "But do tell."

"Traci would be tickled to hear me say your best man is giving me all kinds of Morris Chestnut lusciousness. From the chiseled nose, full lips, rigid jaw line, to his bright white eyes, that man is everything a box of chocolates has to offer. Look at him standing over there looking like he's got me on his mind."

"You know what, Traci was right, you are too much," Brent chuckled. "I have no doubt you're gonna keep us laughing as we all grow old together as friends."

While Brent and I chatted, Traci was off trying to set me up with Steve. Although I wasn't on fiancé patrol I couldn't deny what my eyes were seeing and I thought *He sure is a fine piece of eye-candy. I might have to reconsider.*

When the wedding planner announced "One hour before dinner," our socializing ended abruptly. Time had escaped us all. Steve and I said good-bye with seductive waves and sultry eye contact. The future Mr. and Mrs. Brent swapped hugs. Traci and I hurried to our hotel rooms, showered, changed into semi-formal attire, and made it to the rehearsal dinner with a few minutes to spare.

The rehearsal dinner, a rich soul food spread with all the fixings of a celebratory occasion, knocked me off the diet wagon. I was enticed by a bevy of choices from honey-dipped wings, potato salad, green beans, and candied yams, to banana pudding, pineapple-upside-down cake, and an assortment of decorated cookies and fruit. Pickings were far from slim. I helped myself to some of everything. Weight gain was the least of my worries. My period was a greater concern. It had yet to start flowing.

During the blessing of the food, I craved cramps, bloating and hot flashes and silently prayed *Lord, bring on the curse because I don't want to have a child with Andy if he's not ready!*

13

SCENT-OF-A-WOMAN

Several hours later, my stepsisters checked into the hotel. I put off calling them until the next morning. Attention shifted to the lateness of my period. I was out for blood! Being an unwed mother wasn't on my Bucket List. Another unplanned pregnancy would have been the consequence of relying on the rhythm method—not exactly proven to be a fail-safe method to prevent pregnancy.

Sleepless nights. Soiled baby wipes. Dirty diapers. Bottles mixed with the exact ratio of formula to water, *and* baby daddy drama. "Sheesh!" I sighed. Motherhood was an unconditional responsibility knowing that I was too selfish to sacrifice freedom to meet the demands of parenthood. So, if pregnancy were the result of being irresponsible, an abortion would have been a costly price to pay. I couldn't bear the shame of having the death of another child on my conscience. I had already repented for a previous abortion. I remember exactly the attending nurse's consoling words during that horrible experience.

"The insertion of needles is necessary to dilate your uterus. It's going to pinch a little. Take deep breaths and try to relax. We'll take good care of you." She assured me.

Minutes after the procedure, I was laid up in the recovery room nibbling on crackers, and sipping Ginger Ale with a hot water bottle resting atop my belly. I felt guilty of fetal homicide. Andy was my accomplice whether he knew it or not.

The night our child was conceived the sky was dark with one twinkle of a star watching over me. The moon was unseen. I didn't break my neck to find it. Like love, I knew it wasn't too far away. "One day", I mumbled as I patiently waited for Andy to round the corner of my street in his car, kitted-out with flashy chrome rims and a thumping sound system.

My hair was big and saturated with setting lotion. My sleeveless shirt suffocated my perky tits. I purposely didn't wear a bra. The air was too thick for layers. My skirt was mini, barely there and practically miniscule. My sandals were stacked inches from the ground. Self-confidence gave me all the balance I would need. My skin smelled of berry-scented body splash. My panties were held together by a single piece of material. I was donning a satin thong. Andy greeted me with a suspicious hello and a sinister smirk to my appearance. We were off to dine at a restaurant of his choosing.

Later at his apartment, I understood why Andy didn't comment on my hair, my tits, or my scent-of- a-woman— he was secretly planning an unforgivable assault on my Lady.

First, we started kissing and gently caressing in the front seat of his car. Minutes later, we wound up on his bed slapping bodies to Maxwell's sultry crooning. Andy's hands were busy. One caressed my tits while the other tugged at my thong. His penis was hard. Lady was tense and wet behind Andy's raging hormones. In hindsight, we should've played DMX instead.

Eight weeks later my reproductive chamber was prodded and pricked by multiple needles: one to numb the pain and one to dilate my uterus. In a matter of minutes, I was pregnant no more.

When I left Unplanned Parenthood in tears and riding home in a taxi, I leaned on scripture for understanding what I had just done, *There is a way that seems right . . . but in the end, it leads to death.*

14

THE REUNION

The wedding day had finally arrived. I woke up feeling sluggish but I didn't have the luxury of hitting the snooze button, seeing that I had spent a lot of money to witness Traci and Brent's holy union. Plus it was too late to wimp out on Traci. She needed all the support she could get from her bridal party. While Traci prepared to tie the knot, I prayed for my period to flow, and psychologically prepared to meet my stepsisters. There was no turning back for any of us.

※

Shelly, April, and Candace agreed to meet in the hotel lobby. I was uneasy and somewhat apprehensive about bonding with them, seeing that the last time they were in my company I invited them to kiss my ass. In the years gone by, we were re-acquainted through numerous emails in spite of my rude city ways.

When my stepsisters arrived upbeat and showing me lots of love with smiles and hugs, my nerves were cast aside.

I easily recognized Shelly from the pictures she had sent months prior. April and Candace weren't even a blur in my memory. I had hoped to spare myself the embarrassment of guessing wrongly their identities, but jinxed myself, guessed wrong, and felt like a total idiot for doing so. I guessed Candace to be April because of Candace's style and maturity. Before Daddy passed away, he called out the blue to have our father-daughter-talk; and, from what I recall, other than him being proud of me, was his request for me to connect with Candace. He thought she reminded him most of me. Neither Candace nor April appeared to be offended by my ignorance, or at least that's the impression I got from their body language.

Our reunion started anti-climatic given that we had been counting down the days, weeks, and months leading up to the occasion. The ice had already been broken by way of email.

We hit the ground running. For starters, we enjoyed a continental breakfast in the hotel dining room where I presented them with Boston souvenirs, the closest any of them had been north of the South. I chose the perfect colors. Shelly liked orange so I gave her a fancy candleholder with orange sand and white seashells. Candace's passion for red was inspired by her interest in pledging a popular African-American sorority. I gave her a bottled letter with red sand and vibrant seashells. April got the standard t-shirt.

During breakfast, we proudly talked about our many nieces and nephews and the quirky kiddie things they do, and the darnedest things they say. Our conversation turned serious and shifted to what we hoped to do with our lives—since we were no spring chickens. Shelly was an aspiring chef. April majored in journalism. Candace studied fashion design and marketing. And me, I was on a mission for inner peace. Still,

I was proud of them for following in my academic footsteps. In some strange way, they validated my bachelor's degree. It meant so much more to me. Daddy would have been proud to see me walk across the stage to receive it. He would have been equally proud to hear his daughters engaged in a civilized conversation that had nothing to do with my ass.

The reunion was shaping up to be a moment to cherish. It was clear to me that, time spawned maturity and unity was our destiny.

Following breakfast, we indulged in a little shopping. Sweet on impressions, April surprised me with a pair of sterling silver earrings in the checkout line. She remembered what I liked, too.

Short on time, I had to return to the hotel by 2 P.M. to dress for the wedding. Luckily for the girls, Traci had room for three more guests, due to last-minute cancellations. I didn't have to suggest a gift; they had one when they arrived. I admired them even more for having class and their own common sense. We snapped a few pictures, traded hugs, and planned to meet up again at the reception.

15

TO GOD BE THE GLORY

Traci's wedding day could not have been more beautiful. The sun was shining. The sky was blue with no fluffy clouds in sight.

One by one, each bridesmaid arrived in the hotel lobby. Our full-length, magenta-colored gowns flattered our mixture of apple, banana, pear, and hourglass figures. Traci was radiant in her elegant white lace gown. Overwhelmed by lights, cameras and too much attention, she took cover in a corner of the lobby as we waited patiently to board the limousine.

As the driver approached the church, guests gathered on the front steps to get a glimpse of the bride and her glamorous court. We emerged from the limousine with style and grace. Pandemonium set in. Guests went wild for pictures, bumping each other aside, and calling out "Over here." "This way." "One more. Just one more."

Brent's eyes filled with tears as Traci walked down the aisle, trailed by her stunning dress train adorned with crystals.

In the midst of the excitement, things got dicey inside my stomach. It did summersaults, and turned over everything I had eaten in the last 24 hours. Feeling lighted-headed and queasy, I sat in the church foyer after the ceremony thinking, *This can't be happening, not during Traci's wedding.* A woman passed by carrying a screaming baby. I didn't ask if everything was all right or if I could be of assistance because I wasn't all right and needed moral support. Eventually, she hushed the little one with a binky. At the same time, guests were heading in my direction waving cameras, calling on me to pose for pictures. The look on my face must've given them my answer because they quickly grabbed a different bridesmaid and went on with their business. I was relieved because I was in trouble in the Lord's house and none of them could help me.

Slowly, I was losing faith in prayer and all of its powers to deliver me from the miserable symptoms of pregnancy. I clutched my stomach, and nearly ran to the restroom in need of some space, peace, and quiet. The sitting area of the women's restroom was decorated with a soothing Parisian flair. A floral arrangement was offset by Queen Anne style chairs, while mauve and beige wallpapered walls complemented a gold leafed mirror. I was curious if the men's room was as nicely decorated and then I wondered why I was thinking about that when I should have been worried about an unplanned pregnancy with a man too far removed from his emotions to love me back.

I scurried to the sink and splashed cold water on my face. Then I headed into the stall and almost tripped over my dress maneuvering it to pee. I thought I had peed myself, when I felt a trickle down my inner thigh. When I looked down I noticed that my period had started. I was relieved to be wearing knee-his instead of pantyhose. I wanted to yell, To God Be the Glory, but instead I silently thanked him for looking beyond my faults and seeing only my needs.

16

DEEP CHOCOLATE SKIN

Traci and Brent's wedding reception was held at a swanky country club with cascading waterfalls, exotic greenery, and marble floors. The bridal party arrived long before the bride and groom. The wedding planner escorted us to the formal dining room. Guests found their way to their respective tables. Music played softly in the background. White gloved servers dressed in all black attire served hors d'oeuvres. The bridal party paired up for the formal entrance to the dining room. I sashayed my shapely frame into the great hall swinging my hips wide and loose. I was happy that I wasn't pregnant.

Traci and Brent made a grand, red carpet entrance through the side door into the dining room and then they jumped the broom. Jumping the broom was a symbol of reverence for a slave matrimonial tradition. Traci and Brent jumped into marriage with both eyes open, and since they both jumped the highest, I assumed they would both wear the pants.

Shortly after their arrival, we posed for professional photos, and then transitioned to the traditional first dance. Then it was finally time for dinner. Guests patiently waited to be served a mouthwatering menu of filet mignon, sautéed vegetables, bliss potatoes, French bread, and a spinach salad. On the way to my seat I stopped at Traci's chair.

"Guess what." I whispered.

"What?" She asked curiously.

"I got my period."

Traci's reaction was probably more shocking than Brent's marriage proposal. "Missy, is there something you forgot to tell me?"

"Oh, yeah, I was worried that I might be pregnant with Satan's baby."

Traci chuckled, "Well, maybe you and Steve should hook up, now that you're not knocked up."

Steve's eyes had been following me the entire time we'd entered the hall. As I got closer to my seat, he made his desire known.

"Save a dance for me."

"The last one?"

"That would be special."

"Until then..." I said.

Steve shook his head, and smiled.

Flirtatiously, I walked away with a little extra sway in my hips.

After dinner I checked in on my stepsisters. I barely had a chance to speak to them all day. Candace, April, and Shelly were dancing and enjoying themselves mingling with the crowd. The girls had no idea as to why I was so chipper. I didn't share my good news with them, fearing they would judge me too harshly. Besides my mother Claire always says, "Everything ain't for everybody" so I kept my business to myself. I knew Traci wouldn't repeat my good news to anyone and I hoped

Brent didn't expect her to share our girlfriend business with him. I made a mental note to check-in with Traci to make sure we were still operating under our roommate code of silence.

At the end of the reception, Steve kissed my hand. "Thanks for the dance. It was lovely. Have a good night."

"You as well," I said and walked away to connect with the girls.Candace and April were dog-tired, they passed on joining Shelly in my hotel room for girl-talk.

Shelly and I relaxed on the bed bridging the past. Not once did we broach the subject of my unfriendly sign language inviting her to kiss my ass. But I was prepared to apologize if the topic came up.

Reconnecting with Shelly was personal, intimate and revealing. I learned that she got married and later divorced her husband of four years. After ending her marriage, Shelly decided to turn her life over to Christ, and fell in love with the Word. She was five years celibate, and counting—I envied her resolve because I'd only been abstinent for a month and it was driving both Andy and I crazy.

A faint knock on my hotel room door stalled our talk. I tiptoed to the door, holding up the hem of my bridesmaid dress to look through the peephole. I was shocked to see Best Man Steve standing on the other side, dressed in what looked like workout gear. He stood there, casually running a hand over his chest as though it was perfectly normal to be at my door. I was tempted to call it a night with Shelly so that I could toy with Steve's manhood. I tiptoed back to the bed and whispered to Shelly.

"There's a fine specimen of a man standing about five-eleven, covered in deep chocolate skin, dressed for a workout."

"Obviously Room 669 ain't the hotel's gym. I think Muscle Man has lost his way." She whispered back.

"Shelly, it's Steve, the best man. Do you really think he's looking for the *gym* knocking at my door? If he came to throw some weight around then a workout is exactly what he's gonna get."

Shelly shook her head and said, "Don't even think about making his booty call a reality." Then she laughed, "He'll go away when he gets tired of knocking. Now let's finish catching up."

Shelly was right. Even though I'd flirted shamelessly with Steve, I didn't have to be at his beck and call. So I ignored him to enjoy more quality time with Shelly. He soon grew tired and went away. Secretly I confessed, *If it were not for my period...*

Afterward, an awkward silence fell over the room. I wondered what Shelly was thinking and how she really felt about me. We were practically strangers. Was she happy to see me and get to know me? Would she trust me with more intimate details of her life? Would she confide in me?

I had so many questions about Daddy's death. It had been about seven years since he passed away and the circumstances around his death were still sketchy. Hoping for closure I wanted answers from Shelly since she'd lived with him during his final days.

"Shelly, can you tell me what killed Daddy?" *Damn. What kind of question was that? I'm talking about Daddy like he was a wild animal, or something.* I took a deep breath and tried again. "Shelly, I meant to say, there was some speculation about drug abuse, cancer, and depression. Is there truth to any of this?"

"Simone, let me clear things up. Daddy died of liver cancer. He'd been in and out of the hospital for chemo treatments. He smoked pot every now and again, but I think smoking was a way to numb his pain. He died a slow, agonizing death six months after his diagnosis. Nobody really knew how long he'd been suffering from cancer because he kept everything to himself."

I nodded. "Daddy was always very stubborn."

"He sure was. And telling him what to do in his house—or anywhere else for that matter—was like writing your own death sentence. He wouldn't hear of it. He knew it all and then some. I know I'm wrong for talking about a defenseless man, but this is the only time I can speak freely without him butting in with his fifty-cents."

"Shelly, it's best to let it out. I have one last question, if that's all right with you." I said searching my suitcase for something to change into.

"Sure." Shelly said, standing to stretch her arms and legs. She then sat back on the bed.

"What about the depression?" I asked, easing out of the dress and slipping into Capri pants and a t-shirt. "I can't imagine what he went through was easy, even for someone as resilient as Daddy."

"Simone, this is all true, but when Daddy took sick, his pride suffered, too. He had no choice but to find steady employment that offered an insurance plan that covered pre-existing conditions.

"In the end, I guess a man had to do what a man had to do. So, what was it like living with him during his last days?"

"Mom and Daddy weren't getting along very well by then. We were all walking on eggshells around the house. We tried not to upset him. If we did, our bags had better been packed and ready to go because he would've told us to get the hell out of his house."

Shelly paused for a few moments. I could tell it was hard for her to go on. I can't imagine how hard things had been for them. I remembered living with Daddy. He had a bad temper that anything could set off. My mother Claire was a smart woman the day she packed us up and boarded a bus, Northbound. She never looked back because we deserved a life free of humiliation and random violence. Shelly and I sat quietly taking in the vague chatter outside my door. I wondered if Steve was scheming his next move, then Shelly picked up where she'd left off.

"Like I said before, in the end Mom and Daddy weren't getting along very well. They were both angry and resentful. Daddy was mean and surly without provocation and made his intimidating presence known every waking morning. He found fault in everything from lights being on two seconds longer, to the number of times we flushed the toilet."

I couldn't help but laugh. Shelly, Daddy had a flush counter?"

Shelly joined in with laughter, "No, but he might as well had had one, because he darn sure was keeping count. He even got upset because Mom started working overtime to help make ends meet after he took sick. He swore she had a man on the side. One day Mom came in late from work and was fixing dinner. Daddy grabbed the first thing he got his hands on, that day it was a broken chair leg, and whacked Mom across the arm. She screamed so loudly I ran into the kitchen. A pot of water she had boiling on the stove spilled on the floor and burned her." Shelly was trembling from the memory. "That cruel man didn't even care. He calmly went to his room, but not before telling her to clean up the mess she made and to call her boyfriend to come see about her. Imagine that. The mess *she* made. I knew then that we had to go. Mom grabbed whatever she could carry and got us out of that house. We left before Daddy's health deteriorated." Shelly shook her head sadly. "There wasn't really much we could do for him. He made it so hard. He didn't want us caring for him or comforting him. I think it made him feel weak."

Tears welled in my eyes and slowly flowed down my cheeks. I didn't know if I was sad because I didn't see Daddy in his final hours, or at the thought of him dying a bitter, lonely broken man. So, I attempted to defend his character.

"Shelly, you know Daddy was a prideful man, the ruler of his castle, and not capable of understanding any other way of life—"

"Simone, I can't argue against his pride, but he was a surly, mean old man. He lost his ability to reason along with his hair, weight and appetite. I remember Daddy lying in his hospital bed with tears streaming down his face breathing his last breaths. I don't know how he felt about his older children not being there for him but I think the absence left him really torn up inside."

"Shelly, Daddy was no stranger to me even though we weren't close. The love between us had its limits for sure, and that was mostly his fault, but you know that. A couple months before Daddy took his last breath, we talked about my future, mostly about my unfinished degree. He encouraged me to go back to school. It was important to him that I finish what I had started. He said no job should be left undone. In my heart, I knew Daddy loved all of his children dearly and wanted nothing but the best for us. I believe he found peace for abusing our mothers and breaking up our families. He told me he respected my mother for having the courage to leave the abusive relationship and thought she did a fine job raising us without him. I'm sure he felt the same way about Juanita. After our talk I forgave Daddy because I didn't want him to die feeling that he had failed us or without me saying good-bye."

When I finished speaking there was silence for a long time, then Shelly hugged me and I knew that we would be okay.

Before she left, Shelly's parting prayer was the scripture *Honor your father and your mother, so that you may live long in the land the Lord your God is giving you.*

That night when I finally got into bed, I closed my eyes thankful that my mother did not look back.

17

KISS OF DEATH

As the wedding party made final arrangements to check out and return to their respective homes, Traci and Brent were headed to the Caribbean for their honeymoon.

I had a wonderful reunion with my stepsisters. Over the course of the weekend, we talked, laughed, shopped, and bonded. We planned to spend our last day reliving our childhoods at a local theme park.

For the first time during my trip, I thought about calling Andy. I couldn't wait to tell him all about the good times I was having. I also needed him to pick me up from the airport.

Not sure of the reception I'd get from him, I nervously pressed Andy's number on my cell phone. While the line rang, I had reservations about starting a conversation that might lead to an argument and ruin the rest of my trip. For that reason I thought about hanging up. I feared Andy wouldn't be happy hearing from me, in fact I knew he wouldn't be thrilled to hear my voice after a few days of no contact. Since Susan couldn't pick me up, I had no choice but to contact Andy with hopes of a civil conversation and him agreeing to meet me at the airport.

He answered my call on the third ring.

"Remember me?" I teased, hoping that a game of "guess who" would break the ice.

"Well, look who remembered me. It's been about, what, three days since we last spoke?"

"Andy, please let's not fight. I'm calling you now."

"That was thoughtful, days later."

"My phone rings too if you want to go there with the guilt trip."

"We're even then. So, are you having fun without me?"

"I'm enjoying my sisters."

"Did the groom show up for his wedding?" Andy joked.

"Yes and he's the kind of gentleman I would want my daughter to marry."

"How are you gonna get pregnant if you won't give me any pussy?"

"Listen. I didn't call to talk about sex. Can you pick me up from the airport tomorrow?"

"It's gonna cost you."

"I can only afford to say thank you with a hug."

"That'll do."

"I'll be arriving on flight 1969 from Tampa at 4:30 P.M. tomorrow." I then smacked a kiss of death at the receiver, and dashed off to meet my sisters.

I resigned from calling them my stepsisters and acknowledged them as my sisters. They were respectful, as was I. They were forthright, as was I. They had a sense of humor, as did I. They took their walk in Christ seriously, as I was learning to do. They treated me with genuine love and affection. Most of all, my sisters embraced me as their blood sister; after all we shared the blood of our father. Bonding with them felt special. I wanted to freeze our moment in time, but I never got my way when I wasn't in control of the script. They each had personal agendas. Unfinished business with Andy topped my list.

My sisters insisted on driving me to the airport. On the drive there we agreed to not let years put space between us again. We promised to keep the lines of communication open by phone, email, and even snail mail.

I invited them to visit Boston, and suggested they come during the spring or summer seasons to steer clear of something I still hadn't gotten used to—New England's frigid winters.

When I was a teenager, I remember lying in bed on cold nights praying for the crisp breeze of spring mornings, and the sizzling heat of summer evenings when it was too hot to sleep with panties on. The coldest days of winter my mother would supplement the low output of heat in our apartment by turning on the stove at full blast. I dreaded the day when she had to rely on the oven to keep us warm. One winter the furnace failed in the middle of the night and the temperature dipped to almost freezing. I knew God was watching over us when the furnace miraculously came on a few hours later. The memory of that cold ass day stayed with me all these years.

At the airport, my sisters and I took advantage of our last opportunity for a Kodak moment by volunteering a pedestrian to snap a group picture.

Sadness set in after our good-byes were said and we went our separate ways. The reality at home couldn't possibly measure up to the incredible weekend I'd just spent with Traci and my sisters. I didn't want to leave the hospitality experienced in Florida. But I was homebound with fond memories to cherish. Inside Terminal C I heard someone singing the theme song to *Annie*. Happiness was around somewhere. The baggage handler shot me a smile that left a sparkle in his eyes. I slowed my pace and saw a young girl, holding her mother's hand and skipping along without a care in the world singing "Tomorrow, tomorrow, I love you tomorrow..."

I remember those days of blind faith. Where had they gone and would they ever return? I thought, as I headed for my gate.

While I waited for my row to be called, the ramp attendant small-talked me about the weather, and my pretty smile. I charmed him with sex appeal that secured me a first class seat on the one o'clock flight to Boston.

18

BEENIE BABY PENIS

Flight 1969 landed safely on the ground, albeit thirty minutes late. I grabbed my travel bag and ran to the passenger pick up area in search of Andy but there was no sign of him or his car. I prayed he hadn't forgotten to pick me up or had left because of the delay. It was hot and muggy and I was thirsty and tired. I looked around in search of a seat, and then heard Andy calling my name.

I scanned the waiting area, but didn't see him. I spun in circles trying to find him. I finally spotted him standing on the pedestrian overpass, still dressed in his grungy work clothes. Andy was fuming when he reached me. The sour look on his face told me that he was in a foul mood. So I diverted attention to my luggage, hoping he would offer to carry it to his car, and he did.

"Babe, why do you have that look on your face. Is everything okay?" I asked.

"And what look is that?" He responded looking away from me.

"The look that says you're in a bad mood."

He didn't respond. The least he could have done was act like he was happy to see me. A welcome home hug or a peck on the cheek would have been endearing gestures, and not too much of a stretch for him. His rudeness rubbed me the wrong way. The homecoming was on its way to regret. But I kept my attitude in check because the only thing I wanted to do was take a hot shower, and find my bed—alone.

"Talk to me. What's on your mind? Something must be bothering you." I asked, trying to make peace.

Andy fired back, "Why are you so concerned now? You didn't care enough to let me know your flight would be late."

"I didn't know until we were circling the airport and I couldn't use my cell phone to call you."

"You probably didn't try. I had a rough day and then I have to sit around waiting for you. This is what I get for picking you up. Now get off my back."

"I'm sorry to hear about your day."

"Just drop it. My car is parked on the top level of the garage."

Andy carried my luggage to his car and placed it in the trunk. He walked to the passenger door, opened it to let me in, and waited until I was seated before closing it. When Andy got in the car, I took a chance and thanked him with a kiss on the cheek. He just grunted and started the car.

Andy navigated the early evening traffic with the finesse of a city driver. After a few minutes he started asking me a barrage of questions. He had an itch and was determined to scratch it.

With a smirk in his lips he asked, "Did you have fun?"

"I had a beautiful time at the wedding and bonding with my sisters. It was all perfect." I answered unenthusiastically.

"Why didn't you call to say you made it to Florida safely?"

"You must have amnesia. I did call you. We talked for a few minutes. Don't you remember?"

"Yeah . . . you're right. You called at the *end* of your trip when you needed a ride from the airport."

"Andy, I'm not on your schedule. I called when I felt like calling. And by the way, my ring finger is short 10-carats of a girl's best friend in case you haven't noticed."

"So you forgot to check in with me, but caught the marriage bug? Huh!" Andy grumbled. "You've got a nerve wanting a commitment when you barely communicate with me."

"Pardon me, Andy, but I don't recall you ever checking in with me when you went out of town on your so-called Disc Jockey Conventions. Oh, and while we're on the subject, you still haven't told me why you didn't give me the telephone number to your hotel room in Las Vegas. What about *that* lack of communication?"

"Why do you insist on living in the past? To be honest Simone, I don't know why I didn't give you the number. I wasn't with another woman, if that's what you're assuming."

"You wouldn't tell me the truth if your life depended on it. And if you were so concerned about me, why didn't you just call me?"

"Simone, I'm not lying, and you can't admit that you were wrong for not calling."

"I didn't ask you to pick me up to argue about what I did or didn't do to your satisfaction."

Andy's negative energy was draining. I shut down mentally. We rode the rest of the way in silence. About fifteen minutes later, Andy turned onto my street. After we parked and went inside Andy found his way to my bed. He quickly undressed and threw his dusty jeans on the floor beside his boots. A few minutes later he was fast asleep. His snoring was my cue to take advantage of him whether he knew it or not. I was more interested in the seven messages flashing on my answering machine. After showering, I crept down stairs and pressed play with the volume on low thinking, *Whatever evil lurks in the dark now lurks in the daylight, which leads me to believe evil Andy never sleeps.*

Message 1:

Hey sexy. You know who this is. Stop being a stranger and call me back.

I wish Mr. Beanie Baby penis would go away.

Message 2:

A hang up.

Message 3:

Ms. Miller this is Primary Care reminding you that you have an appointment on July 5th.

Message 4:

Hi neighbor, this is Miss Bonita. I haven't seen you in a few days. I told Ritchie you must be on one of your secret vacations.

I swear she needs a hobby.

Message 5:

Ms. Miller, this is Home Security Services responding to an alarm on your premises. Please call 1-800-555-SAFE, as soon as possible.

That's odd. Susan never called me with an emergency.

Message 6:

This is Home Security Services calling again. Please disregard the first message. We were able to contact your sister Susan. She accidentally tripped the alarm.

Why am I not surprised?

Message 7:

Ah, Ms. Miller. This is Crown Employment Agency. The client would like to extend your assignment for two more weeks, as we discussed. It's yours if you want it. The hours and pay rate are still the same. Show up on Monday or call back if you are unavailable.

Another day, another quarter.

19

HELP! I NEED ADVICE

I fell asleep the moment I shut my eyes. The next morning Andy was up early to hurry home and get ready for work. He slipped out of bed without saying a word to me, no good morning, how'd you sleep, have a blessed day, nothing. He didn't even close the door behind him when he left.

The meteorologist predicted a steamy day, and the possibility of a passing shower. I searched through my overstuffed closet for something loose and soft to wear. I settled on a long, flattering cotton skirt, a sleeveless cotton blouse, and sandals. Dressed and ready to go, I scanned my Things-to-do list. An entry in my personal planner reminded me that I was meeting my prayer partners Denise and Portia at New Baptist for a concert featuring gospel group Repent. I was looking forward to the concert and their debut CD although I dreaded spending an evening in a building with no air conditioning. But I wouldn't leave Portia and Denise hanging at the last minute, plus I bought the non-refundable tickets. I hoped their outstanding debt wouldn't come between our friendships. I made a note to confirm our plans and to let them know that I'd be happy to accept cash, check, or money order.

A few minutes later I was out the door on my way to my temporary assignment. I arrived at work early and settled into my tiny cubicle. I logged onto my computer, thankful for the high-paneled walls. The partition provided privacy while I slacked off tending to personal business online in between sorting, filing, and shredding company documents. The supervisor rarely checked in with me because my duties and responsibilities were clear and not subject to deadlines or customer satisfaction. The support staff around me was out of earshot. The majority wore headphones and mouthpieces to manage customer telephone inquiries. My temporary space was the perfect corporate oasis.

Before starting the work that I was contracted to do, I decided to check my personal email account. I had several new messages. Shelly sent an inspirational quote, April sent an electronic greeting card, and my faithful Internet Romeo had an inquisitive question on his subject line. But Keisha's S.O.S. subject line in all caps aroused my curiosity, so I read it first.

From: Keisha@gp.drama
To: Simone@gp.drama
Subject: HELP! I NEED ADVICE!!!

Message:

Call me. Pronto! Gordon is really pressuring me to have unprotected sex. I told him no, and haven't heard from him in over a week.

I replied to Keisha's email telling her I would call when it was convenient to talk. I had a serious bone to pick with her. If my memory served me correctly, her condom dilemma with Gordon should have been put on ice long before his disappearance.

On my morning break, I slipped into a conference room and dialed Keisha's office. As the phone rang I braced myself for the drama I knew was coming; it was just a matter of how long she would keep me in suspense. Her line rang twice before she answered.

"Keisha Bailey speaking."

"Guess who?"

"Hey, Simone! Welcome back. How was your trip?"

"Refreshing. I'm on cloud nine, and probably won't come down for another month."

"Did you meet any single honeys?"

"The only honey that caught my eye was the best man, but making out was not gonna happen, besides I got my period."

"Oh damn. I don't mess around when I'm on my period either."

"Nice to know a mistress has standards."

"Simone, you're lucky I love you like the sister that I never had. Otherwise, I would've whooped your snooty ass the first day we met."

"Whatever you say Rocky. Whatever you say . . . Now let's hear what's got you in a panic."

"Gordon is pressuring me to have unprotected sex. I keep telling him no and reminding him that he's married."

"Keisha, he knows he's married. You need to remind yourself of that fact."

"Whatever Simone. Anyway, he called me a week ago to say that he had a medical situation that he wanted to talk to me about but I haven't heard from him since. I'm worried. I called his private line at work but his voicemail is full."

"Thanks to you, right?"

"Not funny Simone."

"I wasn't trying to be. What about his Bat phone, is he answering that?"

"He won't answer. My calls go to voicemail and my texts go unanswered. I would go to his house, but after what he did to me when I called his wife, he'd probably kill me if I showed up at his front door. I think he's looking for a reason to break it off because I'm hesitant about unprotected sex. Simone, what should I do?"

"First, slow down. Put the breaks on. Take a deep breath, and tell me what he meant by medical situation. Did he give you any information at all? Do you think he's knocking on death's door?"

"He didn't give me a clue; and, no, I don't think he's dying."

"Keisha, it could be something minor like a tooth extraction for all you know, but you don't. What about his friends or associates that know about your affair? Can you reach out to any of them?"

"We never mingle outside of the hotel, my apartment, or occasionally dining in the boondocks."

"Have you even met his friends?"

"Not one."

"What about his license plate, did you at least memorize that?"

"Why would I need his plate number?"

"You can have his registration checked by the Detective you had a fling with. What was his name, Officer Cash, something like that, right?"

"That's not funny Simone." Keisha snapped.

"Don't snap at me because you barely know anything about the man you're sleeping with, aside from the fact that he's married. If I were you, I'd triple the condom when screwing him for dollars and designer shoes. And if you French kiss and suck his dick, then you'd better get tested for STDs."

"Tested for STDs?" Keisha repeated. Please don't make me think about something that serious when he could be at the dentist getting his tooth pulled like you said. I just want to hear from him. I'm worried sick."

"Keisha, I don't get it. You're worried about a married man?"

"What's wrong with worrying about someone I care deeply about?"

"Why do you care so *deeply* for a man who pissed on you?"

"Look! I provoked him so I can't hold it against him. He had a moment and has apologized with a dozen roses. Gordon is the first man to ever buy me long stemmed roses."

"Roses and all is forgiven?"

"I enjoy his company, the thrill of our affair, and of course gifts of *my* choosing so that I'm never disappointed."

"You'd rather feel special, than be respected?"

"Stop judging something you don't understand." Keisha snapped again.

"Don't get indignant with me. I'm not the one who went ghost on you or humiliated you at the hotel."

"Simone, seriously, what would you do, if you were in my Jimmy Choos?"

"Get out of them, and burn them quick," I laughed.

Keisha retorted. "There's a place for you in Witch Heaven."

"And you're going to Mistress Hell if you have unprotected sex with that married man. So do yourself a favor."

"What's that?"

"Stop seeing that married man. He lies and cheats on his wife, why wouldn't he lie and cheat on you?"

"Gordon has no reason to lie to me. Plus, he's already cheating with me."

"Keisha, I don't know what hold he has over you, and I know it's not just money. You make enough to spoil yourself. Find someone who values you, or someone who is at least available." I advised and then hung up.

A few hours later, I checked my personal inbox. Unsurprisingly I had an email from Keisha.

From: Keisha@gp.drama
To: Simone@gp.drama
Subject: I HEARD U!

Message:

I appreciate your advice and I heard every word you said. I just need to digest all that has happened and decide what I want to do about it. It's going to be a difficult decision to make. By the way, you haven't been to the City since last year. When are you coming to New York for a visit?

From: Simone@gp.drama
To: Keisha@gp.drama
Subject: WE NEED 2 TALK

Message:

Maybe I can head your way before summer's end. You and I need talk, woman-to-woman.

From: Keisha@gp.drama
To: Simone@gp.drama
Subject: DETAILS PLEASE!

Message:

About what? Fill me in. Give me a hint. Is it something you can say over the telephone? Call me!!!

From: Simone@gp.drama
To: Keisha@gp.drama
Subject: Reply to DETAILS PLEASE!

Message:

YOU!

From: Keisha@gp.drama
To: Simone@gp.drama
Subject: DEAL!

Message:

Okay, gotcha! Hey, your visit is a must. We can window shop on Fifth Avenue, take in a play in the theatre district, and check out this new cigar bar where the wallets are fatter than Gordon's!

From: Simone@gp.drama
To: Keisha@gp.drama
Subject: WORKS 4 ME

Message:

(empty)

A cigar bar? That sounded like a place where wallet-chasers like Keisha went to find rich men. Those establishments represented Money, Power, and Respect. It seemed like Keisha had upped her taste from platinum smiles, to men in finely tailored suits who went on the hunt for female company at a Cigar bar. I bet she couldn't wait to show me her I'm-available-and-will-do-anything-for-a-wallet-outfit.

There was no backing out. I was committed to saving Keisha from self-destruction just like my best friend Cindy saved me from emotional meltdowns over my failed relationship with Clay. It was my turn to Pay-It-Forward by helping

Keisha understand that indulging in another woman's husband for money, designer shoes, and risky sex could leave her emotionally and physically broken in unimaginable ways.

In between managing outdated documents, I revisited my inbox to read emails from Shelly, April, and my ever-faithful Internet Romeo.

From: Shelly@gp.drama
To: Simone@gp.drama
Subject: MISSING U

Message:

Hi Sis. We got our pictures back from the Trip. The group picture at the airport is definitely frame worthy. I will send you a copy next week. We miss you already.

—Luv, Shelly

From: Simone@gp.drama
To: Shelly@gp.drama
Subject: Miss U Back

Message:

Hi Hon. I got one set of pictures back too. The one we took at the reception came out beautifully—we struck a serious pose! Say hello to everyone for me.

—Miss U, S.

From: April@gp.drama
To: Simone@gp.drama
Subject: CAN U SAY PAMPER ME?

Message:

Hey Chick-a-Dee, I'm going to the health spa next week. I will tell you all about it when I get back.

—XO, April

From: Simone@gp.drama
To: April@gp.drama
Subject: I'M JEALOUS

Message:

Have fun and get a back rub for me, too.

—Hugs

Before reading Romeo's email, I sent Traci a welcome back greeting card. She surprised me with an instant reply.

From: Traci@gp.drama
To: Simone@gp.drama
Subject: SIPPIN' on COLADAS

Message:

We're on our way to the Coconut Grove Restaurant for dinner. It's supposed to be the "hot spot" on the island. I heard they have the best curried chicken and potent coladas.

Brent said you had many admirers at the wedding. The groomsmen took a bet you weren't wearing any panties under your dress. I'm scared of *you.*

I might send you a doggie bag and a sip. First, you have to tell me what happened when Steve came to your hotel room wearing his workout clothes, according to Brent.

In case you're wondering, my laptop goes wherever I go.

—C Ya, T.

I smiled on the inside, and frowned on the outside wondering what lie Steve told the fellas. I took a few extra seconds to read what Romeo had to say.

From: InternetRomeo@gp.drama
To: Simmy@gp.drama
Subject: CUM OUT, CUM OUT, WHEREVA
U R!

Message:

Hi Simmy. It's been a long time. I miss hearing
from you. I can't get the image of doing something wet and sexy with you out of my head.
Write back, and don't take too long.

—Romeo

Computer love? I hoped not. I only wanted to chat, have a little
cyber sex, and logoff. Romeo and I never once touched on personal stuff like relationships or sexual preferences. He found me
in a "single but *not* looking" chat room. Cyberspace was my escape
to a world that let me forget where I was and who I was. And since
the Andy matter was heavy on my heart, I was in need of a male's
perspective. Romeo opened the door for me to pick his brain.

From: Simmy@gp.drama
To: InternetRomeo@gp.drama
Subject: 4GIVE ME

Message:

Hey Romeo, Sorry for not writing back sooner.
I was on vacation doing some serious thinking

about my relationship (I guess that answers your question).

Anyway, can you help me? I really need a man's point of view on something. Nowadays, it's so easy to be with someone and still feel LONELY. You see, I don't want to waste time or anyone else wasting my time. I would like to sever ties emotionally for me and physically for him. We don't have any common bonds like children or property, and definitely not bank accounts— every fool has her own sense (smile). Can you serenade me with some skillful words to release me from this emotional roller coaster ride?

—Simmy

Weight on my heart lightened. I couldn't fathom why Romeo wouldn't be truthful in his response; he had nothing to lose unless he started having wet dreams about us meeting at a neutral location.

I signed off whistling, "All work and no play would have made for a boring day."

While prepping to leave work, I phoned home to check for messages. Andy had left one saying he cooked tender haddock, creamy asparagus, and rice pilaf, as a peace offering for dinner. He even planned to top it off with a bottle of aged wine.

How enticing and romantically shocking, I thought suspiciously. *I must be dessert. Nice try Mr. Williams.*

The Gospel concert was the per fect excuse for declining Andy's dinner invitation. Not to mention, I had already committed to Portia and Denise for the evening, and the last time I checked with Portia, we were still on.

My luck wouldn't quit. Andy's voicemail kicked in so I didn't have to speak with him. I left a considerate message about attending the concert and asked him to put my food aside. There was no drama about the matter. I hung up feeling that I would enter the Lord's house free of negative energy. I had a wonderful relationship with my sisters, found a sense of closure about my father's death and was on the way to figuring out my relationship, or lack thereof, with Andy. I felt renewed. Life was good at that moment!

20

SICK FETISH

The temperature was a scorching eighty-nine degrees with no chance of a tropical downpour to cool me off. My cotton ensemble was the perfect choice of clothing to combat the heat. Although I dreaded spending hours in a non-air-conditioned church, the ceiling fans would have to do while I got my praise on at the concert.

I was looking forward to hearing Repent sing inspirational selections from their debut CD, *Rise*. Denise was ecstatic, too. Portia was running late, as usual. "Now where could she be?" I wanted to know while pulling out my cell phone to call Portia. Her cell went to voicemail, so I tried her at home.

"Hello." Portia answered sounding like she was crying.

"Portia. It's Simone. Are you all right?" I asked, and then the line went dead. I dialed back concerned about her.

She answered, "Simone, this is not a good time. I'm. I'm." She sniffled. "I'm not in a good place to talk right now."

"I can tell, you're crying. Something must be wrong if you hung up on me. What happened?"

"You wouldn't believe me if I told you."

"I believe something is bothering you. Are you still joining us for the concert? Denise is already here."

"Not in this condition."

"What condition are you talking about? Come on, talk to me."

"Well, I'm sitting on my couch with an ice pack over a swollen bruised eye."

"What? How'd that happen? Oh my God. Don't tell me Lonnie hit you again!" I asked angrily.

"He not only hit me, he practically punched me across the living room. I bumped my damn head when I fell. I swear I saw stars, lightening, and the moon all in one flash. He had no qualms showing me just how disappointed he was that I wouldn't let him screw me in my ass."

"Next time, tell him to buy a blow up doll to satisfy his sick fetish. And why are you still hanging on to Lonnie?"

"Probably the same reason you're hanging on to Andy."

"Portia that was low."

"I didn't mean for it to be. But Andy puts you through changes, too. You break up and get back together. Make up and break up again."

"Ups and downs are part of a relationship. It doesn't mean you should settle for Lonnie treating you like his personal punching bag. And for the record, Andy has never hit me and I wouldn't stand for it either. Portia, don't get stuck with Lonnie. You just met him. It should be easy to walk away."

"You're right, but I think Lonnie and I need to better communicate our expectations."

"I guess. But he's *always* so damn angry. What's up with that?"

"I think I know where his anger comes from."

"Does you knowing give him the right to take it out on you?"

"I don't think he meant to hit me. It seemed like an impulsive reaction."

"The last time you caught a left hook, *and* a slap across your face with the sole of his sneaker, was that impulse, too? It sounds more like abuse."

"Simone, it's not like it's an everyday thing."

"Every day, one day, some days, once a year, Lonnie needs to keep his hands to himself and you should tell him how the abuse makes you feel instead of making excuses for his abuse because that's exactly what it is, abuse!"

"You're being extreme Simone."

"No I'm not. Portia. I grew up in an abusive household. I know what it sounds like, looks like and feels like. Lonnie is abusive and it's gonna get worse. You need divine intervention. Maybe you should speak with Pastor Jenkins, she would be objective and most importantly spiritually uplifting."

"Let me work this out privately." Portia said, her voice shaky. "Simone, promise that you won't tell Denise about this?"

"Why not? She's your friend and would want to know just like I would."

"But Denise also runs her mouth. The whole church will know before dawn."

"Portia pride should be the least of your worries. I'm gonna pray for you."

"Would you please?"

"Yep. I'm going to pray that you don't forget you owe me for the concert ticket that's going to waste."

"Give it away at the door to someone who needs one."

"That's kind of you. But I still want my money."

"You'll get it."

"Portia, I don't know. Maybe Denise and I should come over or you can come to my house for the night."

"Simone, thanks, but I'm fine. Lonnie's gone. He'll come back after he cools down."

"And then all is forgiven?"

"Simone I really like him and there are things about him that you wouldn't understand."

"I guess that answers my question. It's getting late. I don't want Denise to think I left. I'll check in with you later."

"I'd appreciate that. Hey, I might even show up if I can conceal the bruising with makeup."

"There's no safer place than church."

"Let me see what I can do about my face."

"Hope to see you later. Smooches."

"Smooches."

New Baptist was in full service. The atmosphere was the same as it would be on a Sunday morning. The only thing missing was sophisticated Christians in their Sunday best.

The offering tray grew legs and ran two laps, one for the Pastor's birthday, and one for the Building Fund. Those who could afford to give, gave, and those who couldn't, sought refuge in the bathroom. Denise was generous. She took pride in tithing. *She better save some of her enthusiasm for when it's time to pay her debt.* I thought.

The congregation gave ten percent, blessed the trays and the concert got underway. The vocalists in Repent had a set of lungs to rival the Mass Choir. Their singing and grace brought us to our feet. The ceiling fans must've been on heat sensory timers when they kicked in motion, rotating on high speed. The cool air that crept down my back cooled me off. I needed it because the cardboard fan that I was waving back and forth in front of my face wasn't worth my energy.

The concert lifted my spirits. A feeling of calm came over me. I lost myself in the lyrics, stomped my feet to the beat of the drums, and clapped my hands to the rhythm of the music. I was blessed to be there. Finally, my heart *and* mind were in a secure place.

During intermission I found a quiet corner to call Andy.

"Hello?" he answered right away.

"It's just me checking in. How was dinner and did you save any wine for me?"

"Dinner was dinner, the wine is still chilling on ice."

"Is everything okay?" I asked, knowing from the sound of his voice that it wasn't.

"I'm fine."

"I hope you got my message to save some of that tender meat for me. Of course, you know I mean the haddock, right?"

No response.

"I'll stop by around nine-thirty, if that's okay with you?"

"Simone, why even bother? You don't like to eat that late anyway. Aren't you afraid of gaining more weight? You're looking a little pudgy around the waist these days."

Andy was in a mood all right. I took his rudeness as a cue to cut the conversation short and hurry back inside for the second half of the concert.

"It sounds like I'm missing the show. I'll see you later."

"Whatever."

"Should I go home instead?" I asked, deciding to call his bluff.

"It doesn't matter to me. The food will be here if you show up. It's your call."

"All right, we'll talk more when I get there."

Andy didn't have the guts to tell me to go home. I was sure that he had another agenda. So did I if he tried to take a piece of me that I didn't want him to have.

An hour later the concert ended after an amazing encore performance. Denise and I said a prayer for a safe drive to our destinations. I also prayed for Portia's well being.

"Simone, thanks for buying the tickets." Denise said, handing me her payment. "We've gotta do this more often. Maybe we should hit the mall our next outing."

"I'll pass. I'm on a budget and not buying on credit much these days."

"I know what you mean. Jackson hasn't been closing home sales because he can't stay out of the casino."

"Then maybe you ought to stay away from the mall and start building your emergency fund since your husband's priorities are not one hundred percent at home."

"This is true." Denise agreed. "By the way, what happened to Portia tonight? I thought she would beat me here."

"She never showed up. Don't ask me why."

"That's strange. Did you speak with her?"

"Briefly. Last I heard she was looking for her concealer."

"Her and *that* makeup." Denise laughed. "It's fast-becoming her new best friend."

"And for the wrong reason," I muttered.

"What did you say?"

"Nothing. It was great to see you. It's getting late." I said then hugged Denise. "Andy cooked dinner, so I better get going."

"Really?" Denise was practically giddy. "When did he become Chef Romantic?"

"Tonight and it worries me."

21

SEX-STARVED OCTOPUS

On my way to Andy's I turned off Blue Hill Ave., and turned down a quiet street to change into a fresh thong, skintight jeans, a tube top and high-heeled shoes. I fluffed my hair, then added a stroke of hooker red lipstick—Andy's favorite. I topped off my dressed-to- kill ensemble with a single edged razor blade wrapped in a piece of sponge and safely secured in Lady, and then vowed, "*Hell, if women in South Africa 'take drastic measures to prevent rape', then so shall I.*"

As I sprayed berry-scented perfume on my wrist and neck, light beamed through the rear window. I noticed a man approaching my car with a flashlight. When he shouted, "God don't like ugly. Take that trickin' mess somewhere else." I assumed it was the Neighborhood Watch on safety patrol. I drove off before he could get close enough to read my license plate.

As I turned back on Blue Hill Ave., sirens blared in the distance. Traffic merged to the right lane, and came close to a halt. Flashing lights were getting closer and closer. I thought I was busted for impersonating a prostitute; then an ambulance whizzed by at high-speed, followed closely by a police cruiser. I was relieved as I pulled up to Andy's apartment.

Before I could ring the bell, Andy was at the door. The smell of incense wafted through the air. He stood in the doorway with a bottle of beer in his hand, whistling and thrusting his pelvis back and forth, doing his horny dance in anticipation of make-up sex. But sex wasn't happening that night, or any other night. Celibacy was my new line of defense. After my talk with Shelly it seemed like a wise choice, since I desperately wanted to preserve my dignity.

"Damn, baby." Andy said, and then stopped dancing to greet me. "That lipstick is looking good on you! Wait!" He paused as if he'd had an epiphany. "The deacons let you in church dressed like a tramp?" Andy asked laughing, and then he took a swig of his beer. I smelled it on his breath from where I stood.

"What do you think?" I answered.

"I don't know. Maybe the deacons liked your look. You don't hear me complaining, do you?"

"Andy for your information, I changed clothes *after* the concert." I said rolling my eyes at him.

"Don't roll your eyes at me. The deacons could've been sweet on you tonight, that's all I'm saying. I hear most deacons are players." Andy laughed and took another swig of beer.

"It takes a player to know one."

"Now, now, now. Let's not waste time arguing. Get your pretty self in here before I lock you out."

I turned around and walked to my car.

"Simone, where are you going? I know you're not going home looking like a lady of the night. You must have somebody else waiting for you."

I stopped and turned to look back at him.

"Why, you lousy son-of-a . . . Never mind. I'll let that one go. My spirits are too high right now to let you clip my wings."

"Oh forgive me. I almost forgot that Miss Goody Two-Shoes got her praise on tonight," Andy said looking at his watch, "Let's see how long your good girl act lasts."

"You're such an asshole Andy. I don't know what I was thinking coming over here." I said heading back to my car.

"Wait. I didn't mean it. Simone, please don't go!" Andy shouted. His voice was loud enough to wake the dead resting in the cemetery across the road.

"I'd rather take my act somewhere else than waste it on you."

"You know something, Simone. You are a sensitive bi—"

When I heard the B-word about to jet from his mouth, I ran back to confront Andy like I could take him on and win. I dared him to man-up and speak his drunken mind so I could scratch my initials across his face as a permanent reminder of what the bitch in me could do.

"What's the matter, Andy? Are you at a loss for words? Do you need help insulting me? Let's hear it!" I screamed.

"Simone, stop making a scene."

"Whoa! You've got nerve expecting me not to embarrass you as much as you act a complete fool inside and outside my house. So spare me! I'm going home and won't be coming back. Don't call me and I damn sure won't call your disrespectful ass!"

"Simone don't go. We need to talk."

"About what, being just friends again?"

"Trust. I don't trust you. You're always making plans around me, taking trips that don't include me and when you get back, you're so cold to me. I can't even touch you."

"Andy lies, lies and more reverse psychology lies. You knew about the Florida trip. You tried to rape me before I left, remember? And please stop blaming me for living my life. I plan around you because you choose to make yourself unavailable to do anything that even sounds like a commitment. Lately, the only things you seem to be interested in are sex, sports and beer. What happened to the Andy I fell for, the compassionate Andy, who made me laugh? Did he ever exist?"

"Of course, and I'm still here."

"Then the least you could do is show some interest in this so-called relationship beyond the bedroom. I'm more than the 'sexy pussy" between my legs. My idea of romance is not just a surprise dinner, or a night out on the town just so you can demand sex in return."

"Simone, what do you want from me?" he sighed.

"Andy, I want to know if we are in a relationship because lately when we are so-called together, I feel lonely, but when I'm away from you, I feel alone. And I didn't come here for you to call me a bitch! Let's start with you respecting me. But, if you want to end this relationship, or whatever you're calling it tonight, you can stop pretending and put *your* act to rest!" A storm brewed inside me. I wanted to scream and curse Andy at the same time, but I didn't let him break me emotionally. I refused to shed another tear. "You know what, Andy? Coming here tonight was a big mistake. I'm not even really sure why I'm here. I'm going home. Besides you've been drinking and the beer has been doing most of the talking tonight."

"Simone, calm down and hear me out. I love you too much to lose you. Come inside so we can talk. And you must be starving. Don't let a good meal go to waste."

Hunger and poor judgment led me inside. The kitchen was filled with the pungent scent of freshly minced garlic. My mouth watered, and my eyes filled with tears when I saw the table set for a party of one. Vanilla scented tapers burned dimly in its center. A wine glass, cloth napkin, and a knife and fork were laid out. In the middle was a plate of creamy asparagus and haddock on a bed of rice. I didn't know what to say. The beautiful meal was more than I'd done for him over the past six months. I felt terrible for scolding him.

"Andy, I can't believe you did all of this for me. I feel so special."

"That's because you are." He wiped my tears, and softly kissed my forehead. "Sit and enjoy your dinner. I'll be right back."

He left the kitchen and went into the living room. I clinked the fork on the side of my glass just to see if it would get his attention. Not a chance. He disappeared out of sight. I stopped the clinking because it was getting on my damn nerves. A few minutes later I heard Andy channel surfing with the volume on high. He settled on his favorite show, *Sports Center Live*. As usual, sports came first over spending quality time with me.

I didn't understand. Why go to so much effort just to ignore me? "Whatever," I sighed and picked up my fork and ate the delicious meal. I left the wine untouched. While eating, I heard Andy grumble about the sports replay. We never had the talk he was so anxious for. I crumbled up the napkin and tossed it across the table, then slowly devoured more food. I chased it down with ice water. In between burps, I heard the sweet sound of snoring. That was my signal to cover up the leftovers with aluminum foil and place them in the refrigerator. After washing the dishes and cleaning up, I blew out the candles and pondered whether I should drive home, or spend the night. The clock struck midnight. I was spent. The humidity drained what little energy I had left.

Fatigued, I decided to spend the night thinking that maybe I could persuade Andy to cook a down-home southern breakfast in the morning: *Fish, grits, and a hot cup of decaf would settle our differences. Maybe.* I hoped. In the bathroom I removed the razor blade and wrapped it in my thong, and then I took a soothing shower that washed away the sticky residue from the humid day. Feeling fresh and smelling clean, I eased into bed not at all surprised to see that Andy was already there. I closed my eyes and prayed for a good night's sleep.

"Mmm. You smell so damn good." Andy whispered, nuzzling my neck.

It wasn't long before he was climbing all over me like a sex-starved octopus. I felt his hardness rub up against my thighs. The warmth of his drunken breath irritated the back of my neck. His panting was making my nipples hard; Lady's sugar started flowing. She was wet behind his horniness and wanted his hard penis more than I cared to admit.

Andy sensed that Lady was ready. He slipped his fingers between my thighs and pulled at my thong. Backed up with sexual frustration, he roughly separated my legs. At the same time, I fought desperately to keep him from shoving his stiff penis inside of me. Dripping with sweat, Andy renewed his efforts and was almost at the gate when I purposely rolled off the bed and on to the floor to escape him. Ignoring the pain in my right side, I jumped up, flailing my arms, yelling at him to get control of himself and his dick. Andy rolled over and laid with his back to me for the rest of the night.

Setting parameters empowered me to stay in control of my body, and keep my dignity intact. That night I claimed victory. Or, so I thought.

22

GUILTY

The next morning, I walked into the bathroom and saw that Andy had politely packed up all my personal belongings and placed them on the towel shelf. Once I'd gotten my head around that, my attention shifted to my crusty ass cheeks that were stuck together.

As I stared at my crusty butt in the mirror, Andy was knocking on the bathroom door. He'd have to wait. A serious body check was in order.

I touched the dried white substance, then turned on the vanity light and gave it a closer inspection. It was dry and flaky and it had a faintly recognizable smell. "Wait a minute. It smells like... semen," I fumed and didn't want to believe my eyes or my nose upon learning that selfish Andy had masturbated in the middle of the night and left his dried sperm smeared over my butt cheeks and between the crack of my ass. I understood that Andy was horny, but, taking what he wanted while I slept was going too damn far.

Feeling soiled and dirty I turned on the shower in an attempt to wash away Andy's selfish deed and restore some of my self-esteem. As I stepped under the water I thought back almost two years ago to another one of Andy's deeds that should have set me free of him.

This shocking revelation of his DNA on my ass ranked almost as high as when I found hair in his bed, hair that hadn't come from my head. That discovery left me wanting to curse Andy out for the cheating bastard that he was but I kept quiet and made it another reason to justify my sworn abstinence. I chose not to confront Andy about it because I didn't want him to deny it and try to deceive me from another angle in the future; and, truth be told, I wasn't ready to be single again.

While I was in deep thought, Andy started banging on the bathroom door. I suspected his patience had shortened to a candlewick. But I didn't care if he pissed his pants. I was lost in memories of troubled times between us and I started to hate Andy for not walking out of my life a year ago when he all but confessed to being commitment-phobic.

One Saturday afternoon, he called to say he wanted to talk about something very important. He even made an appointment to meet with me later that evening, but refused to give me a hint over the telephone. He said it wouldn't have been fair to me. My heart hit the floor. I suspected long before his call that he struggled with his emotions. Part of me feared the inevitable pressure of commitment was finally getting to him.

Like many other times during our turbulent relationship, we weren't seeing eye to eye—get the hell out of my sight, I can't stand you, was more like it. Still, I chose to be patient while Andy grappled with his commitment issues. I wanted to believe that fate brought us together. But I was wrong and deeper in denial. Maybe fate did bring us together but sex kept us going, and going, and going, more so for his pleasure than mine.

When Andy came over to talk that Saturday afternoon I made a conscious decision not to wear anything provocative. So I wore loose fitting jeans, and an oversized sweatshirt.

When Andy walked in I led him to the sofa. I cut to his chase, and asked if he wanted to end the relationship. That day I needed closure but that's not what I got. Instead Andy said, "Sweetheart, you are the best thing that has happened to me, and I have no doubt that you can make me happy. I thought I could settle down, and if I choose anyone it would have to be you."

Choose, echoed in my head.

"Simone, my family has a history of failed marriages and I don't want divorce to be our outcome. I want a marriage that will stand the test of the worse times."

Family history? I never figured Andy to be a coward. I would respect him more if he had just admitted to being commitment-phobic.

"Sweetheart, you're beautiful on the inside and on the outside," Andy continued.

I guess he thought I was a sucker for flattery, too.

"I wouldn't be honest if I didn't say you can be wicked at times, but I think I'm to blame for some of it."

Think?

"Simone, what I'm trying to say is that I don't want to lead you on, only to let you down in the end."

I did not respond.

"Sweetheart, please tell me what you're thinking. I know you must think I'm a jerk, and I am."

Finally, the truth for once.

"Simone, I care deeply for you. I don't want to hurt you because you deserve happiness."

I sat silently in a daze. It took all of my strength not to unravel emotionally. My self-esteem was hanging on by a single thread.

Andy eased closer to me and placed his arm around my neck.

"I'm sorry I took you for granted all these years; I thought I'd be ready to settle down, but I'm not. Will you ever find it in your heart to forgive me?"

I pushed his arm away and stood up. I walked calmly upstairs to my bedroom, closed the door behind me, undressed and got into bed. A few minutes later Andy made his way upstairs. I pulled the covers up to my neck, closed my eyes, and prayed for him to go away and let me grieve in peace; but he didn't. He let himself in and stood at the bed asking if he could hold me one last time. Mistaking my silent anger for an invitation, he undressed and got into bed mostly to rub his penis against my ass once more for the road.

Night turned to morning. When I woke, Andy lay sleeping like the devil's angel. I quietly hummed the lyrics of "Guilty" because either we were two fools in love or just too used to one another to walk away. That was one year ago—my formal induction into Hopeville.

Since then, not much had changed. It was time to make things right. It was time to face that lying emotionally manipulative, booty violator. I had a graveyard of bones to pick with Andy—my crusty ass cheeks for one—and I was ready to start digging. I got out of the shower, dried off and slipped on Andy's t-shirt that was hanging behind the door.

I opened the door and faced him. "We need to talk."

"Sweetheart, here you go getting all tense again. Loosen up and laugh a little."

"I stopped laughing a long time ago."

"I thought we squashed that argument last night?"

"Not, 'we', *I* resolved the matter by myself. You fell asleep while watching TV. Of course, you wouldn't remember. You were drunk."

Andy inched closer trying to grab my waist, "Let me fix you breakfast. We can make-up afterwards." He said and then started running down his menu: "Home fries, wheat toast, cheese eggs and grits. I bet you thought your man didn't remember what his woman likes, huh?"

"This is your MO isn't it, Andy? Pretending you care until you get what you want. You've been doing it our entire relationship."

"So, can I take that as a yes or a no for breakfast?" Andy asked avoiding the question.

I pushed him away, crossed my arms, and demanded, "Tell me what went on behind my back and between the crack of my ass while I slept last night?"

Andy turned away.

"Face me so that we can deal with this issue."

"Come on now sweetheart. Why are you trippin' so hard this morning? Will you lighten up, please?"

"No. I will not lighten up. I want to know what happened and why?"

"Isn't it obvious? I wanted you and you turned me down. Do you have any idea what it feels like to have a dick as hard as wood lying next to some sexy ass pussy? You can't hold out on me forever. Lately you've been pushing me away, like your heart is somewhere else. Is it? Tell me so I know where we stand."

"Andy, don't guilt-trip me with your reverse psychology. What you did was wrong. It had nothing to do with me. Jacking off on me was disrespectful."

"Woman, you had me all backed up. Your body smelled good. I thought you wanted me, too. What else was I supposed to do knowing the sexy pussy you got between your legs was thirsty for me? Tell me it wasn't."

"Don't worry about what's between my legs. It belongs to me, not you. Next time, try a cold shower and take your penis rubbing ass to sleep."

"Simone you're not exactly innocent."

"I didn't make you violate me."

"You set me up."

"How so?"

"You came here last night wearing the bait."

"What *bait?*"

"You know that red lipstick and berry scented perfume turn me on."

"That's a lame excuse for violating my body."

"I'm not finished telling you how you set me up."

"Go on."

"When you got into bed you smelled so good and you turned your back to me like you were ready for me."

"Andy, your selective memory is amazing. I practically fought you off last night and threw myself on the floor to get away. What you did while I slept only proves that you're sick and can't be trusted."

"Sweetheart, let me make it up to you. Just tell me how and I'll do it." Andy reached for my hand. I pulled it back.

"Sorry, but I can no longer forgive your sins against me. Last night you crossed the line. Your selfishness ends today!"

23

UNFORGIVEABLE

Whilе Andy used the bathroom, I got dressed. When he came out a few minutes later he made a play for retaliation by announcing his Fourth of July plans that didn't include me joining him at a family cookout on a beach, south of Boston. If I couldn't be by his side, I settled for being with him in spirit, bad spirits.

"Do you intend to be there all-day and overnight, too? And why am I just hearing about the cookout?" I questioned him.

"Yeah and stop pretending you didn't know just to start a fight to keep me from going. I mentioned it before you went to Florida."

Since lying and cheating go hand-in-hand, I pushed the issue further.

"You never told me about it. What do you suggest I do while you're off celebrating?"

"Who said anything about celebrating? Our ancestors were beaten and chained on slave ships crossing the Atlantic Ocean. They weren't celebrating fireworks, they were raped, and the weak were fed to sharks. Plus, I'm not in a hurry to be around my drunken family. I'm just going because I have the day off from work, I don't get many. And since we're on the subject of having fun, where are your church-going girls? I'm surprised you didn't make plans with them."

"*My* girls? Where's *your* girl, at home getting all jazzy for your little family picnic?"

"You're my only girl." Andy said trying to pull me closer to him.

"Am I, really?" I asked swatting his hands away.

"Are you having doubts?"

"I have reason to believe you've been unfaithful."

"Be careful not to confuse your emotions with facts. You might jump to an embarrassing conclusion."

"Thanks for the warning, liar."

"Don't mention it."

"Fess up, Andy. Who is she?"

"Change the fucking subject and stop nagging me. I made dinner for you last night and you were late."

"Andy, you're full of it. You knew about the concert. God help me, I don't know why I put so much energy into a relationship that isn't worth it. Fine. Go without me. I hope you and your girlfriend have fun."

"Simone, I'm warning you, stop accusing me of something you can't prove. I've had enough of your whining today."

"And I've had enough of you taking sex from me whenever you want it and not caring how your selfishness makes me feel cheap."

"You know something you little bitch." Andy charged at me. "You're getting on my nerves with your mouth. Either you close it or I'll shut it for you."

Andy was in my face. I didn't back away from him. He wasn't the only one with pent up frustration. I had enough of my own to slaughter a cow.

"Are you threatening me?" I picked up my cell, and punched in 9-1-1. "Make one wrong move to hurt me and I will send your ass straight to jail. My mother was abused by my father, and according to you, your mother got her ass kicked by yours, so if you think for one minute I will stand here and let you put your hands on me, and get away with it, you are gravely mistaken!"

Andy softened his stance.

"I'm not my father, Simone. I would never hit you."

"You hurt me with your mean words, and degrading actions. What you did to me last night was inexcusable."

"But I didn't mean to hurt you." Andy said pulling me close. "I love you and it won't happen again. I swear."

I stepped out of his embrace. "Andy we can't get along for a stretch of three weeks. Maybe we *both* need some time to figure things out."

"No. I don't want to break up. I want to be with you. I love you and don't want to lose you."

"Andy you need to make up your mind about this relationship because I'm sick and tired of you wasting my time. I'm sick and tired of you taking from me. I get tired of waking up with your dick in my back all the time. The sex ain't all that if you really want to know the truth."

"Woman, you better watch what you say to me in my house!" Andy shouted, with a wild look in his eyes, and his hands balled into fists. I could feel the anger radiating from him. After all the advice I had given Keisha, and Portia, I found myself about to become a victim of physical abuse. I stepped away from him and measured the distance from where I stood to the front door in the event I had to run for my life.

I switched to survival mode to get me out of Andy's apartment—alive. I was closer to the door, so I had the advantage. It made no difference because I was still in harm's way of Andy's fists that were in the same position: balled tight, ready to pounce all over me. In spite of fear, I tried raising my voice as a defense.

"Wait one damn minute! Do you see the words 'abuse me I have low self-esteem' written across my forehead?"

Andy fists remained balled tight.

I lost the will to fight my way out of a relationship that was doomed from the start.

His actions were unforgivable. I didn't trust him to keep his word to never hit me. That was impossible, physical abuse was in his blood. His father beat his mother and their sham of a marriage ended in a nasty divorce. Strangely, Andy's mother was apathetic towards his abusive tendencies. She once told me that her failed marriage had no influence on his ability to nurture a healthy relationship. She was naïve to think one had nothing to do with the other. She didn't know her son like I knew him—a loose cannon with a short wick, an adverse affect of witnessing domestic violence as a child.

Andy may have started off as Mr. Nice Guy, but over time I knew he wasn't the one for me, especially after what he did to me last night and now physically threatening me. My mind was made up—our quasi-relationship was over.

I prayed for my feet not to fail me as I grabbed my purse and ran for the door, forgetting my overnight bag on the floor near his coffee table. Andy snatched it up with a sneer on his face.

"Relax and take a seat. Don't worry. I'm not going to hit you."

"May I have my bag, please?"

Andy held my belongings close to his chest.

"I'll give it to you after we sit and have a civilized conversation."

"Andy, I should go home now. We can talk later."

"You're here. Let's talk and clear the air."

"Now is not the right time. We're both upset and need some time to think things over, especially if we're going to stay together." I added to sweeten the pot.

Teary eyed, a contrite Andy handed over my bag, and made his case for forgiveness.

"Simone, being horny for you makes me do some crazy things. I was wrong for jacking off on you. Now can we please make love so that I can show you how special you are to me?"

He must be out of his bipolar mind. I thought as I ran out the door to save my life.

24

A CHANGE IS GONNA COME

Feeling safe in the car, I restrained myself with the seatbelt as my gloomy eyes stared back at me in the rearview mirror. The reflection of disappointment weighed heavily on my mind. Instead of peace, I saw misery supported by dark circles that Portia's concealer couldn't hide. My sullen eyes were the result of being emotionally drained in a fruitless relationship.

I stayed outside Andy's apartment a bit longer thinking about the disrespect, and near-violence that took place inside. I glanced over my shoulder at his window to see if he was peeking, secretly plotting his revenge. After all, I knocked his fragile ego down a peg or two. At some point he will try to get it back up at my expense.

Still upset about being victimized, I wanted to even the score and abuse something of value to him. His dusty Cougar was parked in front of my car. I thought about leveling all four tires, scratching hate filled words in the paint from the hood to the trunk, and pouring sugar into his gas tank. Gluing the door locks would have been the ultimate revenge. Andy needed to know that it was in me to be the bitch he was determined to crown me. But I chose to be a bigger person knowing that him being without me would be punishment enough.

My hand fiddled with the buttons on the dashboard. Slowly the driver side window rolled down, without given much thought to my actions, I reached into my purse, retrieved the razor blade and tossed it down a nearby street sewer. Driving away, I declared, "It's onward and upward for me. Time to move on and far away from Hopeville."

I took the scenic route home, and drove up Blue Hill Ave. feeling like the weight of disappointment had been lifted off me as I admired the Mom and Pop stores, and churches of all denominations along the way. I was proud to be part of the up and coming community. Trees and hardy perennials were planted on the route; renovated storefronts were no longer guarded with chain link grates forbidden by law, and trash receptacles neatly lined the streets.

The vibrant scene was a sign that Urban America finally got her facelift. Decades later, Blacks in my community were no longer the underdog race, under-educated, under-housed, or subjected to substandard living conditions. More residents qualified for home loans. Seemingly, red taped disadvantages had finally been severed. Poverty was on the downswing. Gloom and doom was replaced with a strong sense of pride on Blue Hill Ave.

But it would have been premature to rejoice. Black on Black crime was devastating the Black family. The increasing number of liquor stores and fried chicken joints threatened the community's health, along with corner stores that sold potato chips insultingly named Homeboys and Homegirls. Despite socio-economic progress, there was more work to do, undivided. Unity would result from strength in numbers standing in opposition of liquor stores, junk food stores, and fast food eateries. It was time to lobby for salad serving establishments.

One day change is gonna come. I thought arriving home sweet home where I parked in my driveway and sat in the car. My thoughts circled back to Andy, searching for answers to make sense out of what transpired with the man I wanted to love.

I was disappointed in Andy and our relationship. The inevitable bad ending had become a reality. I had to bless and release him from my heart. I knew it wouldn't happen overnight, but I had to start somewhere. Andy was indeed a brazen wolf disguised as my sheep, too far removed from his emotions to love me back. In fact, he loved me not.

After needed reflection, I had to find a discreet way to get inside my house in last night's hooker outfit without Miss Bonita seeing me. To my surprise she wasn't perched in her window yakking on the phone, passing the morning hours catching up on gossip.

I was in luck, and slipped quietly out of the car, careful not to slam the door. My adrenaline was pumping as I hopped the stairs.

Safely inside I paused to reflect some more on the changes I had been going through with Andy. I checked myself before my emotional state spiraled out of control and led me back to him. I had no desire to be superwoman on a mission to save a man from self-destruction. The time had come for me to get on with my life without him. I made an oath to unshackle myself from his heartache and vowed to invest in my personal, social and spiritual growth, with the Lord as the captain of my vessel steering me in the direction of some much-needed retail therapy to take my mind off social drama.

After changing clothes, I was fast out the door and in my car turning the radio dial to the oldies but goodies station. I tuned in just in time to catch the tail end of "Celebration."

Bargain Basement was my first stop. Markdowns were in full effect and I scored big. One thing that had to change was my shopping philosophy: A bargain was no longer a bargain if it left me broke. If I bought a pair of shoes, I purchased a belt and a purse to coordinate with the shoes; otherwise, they were left on the rack. At the end of my Bargain Basement session, I put together a complete outfit, perfectly matched from the skirt down to the shoes. The financial damage didn't break my wallet. I ran up an $80 tab and walked out of the store with some great buys. The skirt! The snug fit! "Hmm . . . Andy would die if he saw me flossing in this red mini and pumps to match. Huh! Not a chance!" I chuckled.

After Bargain Basement, I made a quick stop at Music City and perused the latest Gospel CD releases. I searched for Repent's CD. But chart topper *Rise*, was out of stock so I purchased *Mountain High, Valley Low,* instead.

Leaving Music City, a young thug approached me. Premium chocolate unwrapped ran his fingers through the neatly parted cornbraids, situated row-by-row from the front of his head, to the nape of his neck. Face-to-face, he wasn't shy.

"If a picture is worth a thousand words, then seeing you leaves me speechless. Youngblood."

His confident introduction was a natural turn-on.

Inside my head I said, *Yep, he's jive.* Then I quietly responded, "Hello" and kept walking and smiling my thoughts, *He sure is fine though. I might have to reconsider getting to know my future mistake.*

Still vowing to stay true to myself, I recited Matthew 26:4. *Watch and pray so that you will not fall into temptation. The spirit is willing, but the flesh is weak.*

25

UNTAINTED, GUILTLESS, AND SHY

Maintaining a cordial relationship with my ex-boyfriend Clay had its benefits. Over the years, Clay and I were able to communicate and be in each other's company without the intrusion of intimacy. I couldn't reignite an intimate desire for him even if I was horny enough for a one-night stand. My heart wouldn't let me forget why we broke up. Besides, I moved on, not necessarily to greener pastures dealing with Andy, but being with him helped me forget the bad times Clay and I once shared.

I was fourteen years young when I met Clay. He was a sixteen-year-old teenager who took pride in riding his BMX bike. He could work his handlebars with serious finesse. One day he got carried away and crashed down hard on his private parts. I ran home, got some ice, but didn't do the honors applying comfort. My interest in Clay didn't go any further than his bike riding skills, given that I wasn't remotely in touch with my sexuality yet. I was still a virgin when one of his bike-riding friends nudged us together at a community carnival. It's safe to say I was a kid at heart, untainted, guiltless, and shy.

Clay and I had our time. We really did. We made the best of the good and learned to live with the bad.

Our good was good, and the bad was . . . well . . . bad. The best of the good were spent swinging on playground swings, and sitting on park benches taking in the starlit sky, imagining what our lives would be like ten years down the road raising children, and juggling gymnastics and softball.

We created our own space out of earshot of my mother's discipline calling for me to "Get in this house now!" Sometimes I would ignore her just to sneak in a few innocent touches, I more than he. But I didn't go too far with my curiosity because her chastising words always lingered in the back of my head, "Don't bring home no babies, that's all I've got to say, 'cause I already raised my children and I'm not about to be saddled down with no headaches. And if you start acting grown, you had better look for your own apartment, because two women can't rule the house!"

My mother got on my nerves with that mess. But she was right. I didn't know the first thing about sex or raising babies. Her way of talking about "the birds and the bees" was telling me time and time again, 'don't bring home no babies'. Fresh out of middle school and too young to work, little did she know, I hadn't even had my period yet.

Clay was a junior in high school and more experienced with dating. But he didn't pressure me into sex. He showed me respect, and earned the right to tug on my heartstrings. I was hooked on Clay and didn't fight to free myself. I was in love, or at least it felt that way until he showed me otherwise.

Our relationship changed when the player bug bit Clay. He didn't hesitate to sow his wild oats when he was a freshman in college sporting a brand new, slick BMW M5 with black leather interior, tan piping, and flashy Schnitzer rims to close his rap. Clean as a whistle, trouble-on-wheels attracted every loose woman in its path. I swore he loved that car more than he loved cooked food. In fact, he worshipped the ground it rolled on.

Clay quickly took the lead on the playing field. He went from pulling on my heartstrings, to stomping on my heart.

One night I waited hours on end for him to come home. His mother invited me inside but stubborn me chose to sit on the porch, and froze my tail off.

Cold, tired, and shivering, foolish me trudged an hour away from home wearing nothing more than a thin sweater, a pair of short, shorts and sneakers, just to catch Clay in the act of cheating. Four hours had passed before he finally did arrive home to find me waiting. When I heard reggae music, and smelled the scent of marijuana I knew Clay was coming. I went in full alert-mode, ready to fight without a weapon. I had already figured in my head the poison I would spew when he stumbled upon my presence. I knew he wouldn't be happy to find me on his front porch stalking him either. I didn't give much thought to how I would make him understand that I wasn't unstable. I only wanted his undivided attention—the same attention he gave the car and the skirts he chased. I chickened out when we came eye to eye and fixed my gaze on the intense moon dangling in the sky. I felt crazy for being there. Love had nothing to do with it—I was an insecure mess.

At first, Clay was startled when he saw me on the porch, then he gave me the cold shoulder, scooted pass the lawn chair and went inside. I couldn't believe he treated me with disregard, like I was also a piece of furniture. I got ready to speak, before I could say a word, Clay went inside and slammed the door; that was his way of telling me to shut the hell up, before I went on a warpath. Either it was my imagination or Clay had hot pink lipstick on his cheek. I had hoped Clay's obsession with a flashy car was something that would pass, but it drove him to a new level of disrespect for me. I wanted answers.

I hopped off the lawn chair, and hung on the doorbell.

He opened the door with a wet washcloth in one hand, and a cordless handset in the other, I assumed calling one of his skirts to continue their rendezvous.

"Nervy of you to be on the phone considering I'm the one freezing my ass off, not the skirt you're checking in with."

His glassy eyes pierced through me. Clay kept pressing numbers on the keypad and wiping his cheek clean of lipstick.

"You rude bastard it's too late to wash away the evidence." I cried and slapped the receiver out his hand.

"Are you crazy?" Clay snapped and then hit me with the washcloth. It stung my face.

Without thinking, I punched him in the nose. He lost balance and landed flat on the floor. Seconds later, I was on top of him, biting his ear and digging my fingernails deep into his skin. His stepfather appeared out of the shadows of the dark hallway and pleaded with us to calm down and act like adults. Then he called for Clay's mother to talk some sense into both of us. They struggled to break up our rumble. We found ourselves piled one on top of the other, with Clay appropriately on the bottom. I got up, grabbed the handset, high-tailed it to the bathroom, and pressed redial. A skirt answered. I didn't disgrace myself with name-calling; I chucked the handset into the toilet, darted out the bathroom, and out the front door. Clay didn't budge to stop me.

His only words were, "Be careful going home."

"Forget you. Forget your car! Forget your pink lipstick wearing floozy, and forget my number!" I yelled back with tears raining down my face. I cried more so because I had to accept that an object with four wheels and glistening paint had defeated me. I was humiliated, and cried all the way home, and the tears didn't stop until the sun rose the next morning.

From that day forward, our relationship hit rock bottom.

Instead of giving into Clay's pleas for forgiveness, I declared war on his skirt magnet, and punctured the tires on his most-prized possession. He got revenge where I least expected him to find me. After running up another shopping tab at the mall, I found my sports coupe in a miserable state in the parking lot. The tires had been sliced, leaving me stranded. I knew then I had to either leave Clay, or do time for manslaughter.

In my heart of hearts, there was no future with Clay. I also knew that he wouldn't sacrifice hanging with his friends, chasing skirts, smoking pot and drinking to stifle himself in a monogamous union with me.

When the wheels finally came to a screeching halt, I got off Clay's rollercoaster to ride my own. I had the front seat all to myself, my hands were up, and I loved every minute of it. I had no desire to get close to anyone. I took advantage of free meals with casual dates. My heart was sealed tight until there was no more joy in casual dates.

When it didn't pain me to be without Clay, I gave love one more chance with Andy. It was only by the grace of God that Clay and I resolved to go our separate ways and remain friends in spite of our differences.

After I sent the page my telephone rung. I hoped it was Clay calling, and not Andy. I stumbled running for the phone and stubbed my pinky toe. The accident was good for about thirty seconds of swearing. When I answered, Clay's low, smooth Caribbean voice filtered through the receiver.

"Simone, what's up? Is something wrong?"

"No. I was just wondering what you're up to."

"You were thinking about me at this hour of the night? I find that hard to believe. Where's your boyfriend?"

As a rule, I didn't discuss past lovers with present lovers, and vice versa. Nothing good would come from it. I talked around the question.

"We're not discussing him. Where are you?"

"Not far."

"Come over."

"Are you sure your boyfriend won't mind if I stop by?"

"I don't answer to him."

"Oh, that's right. I forgot I'm talking to Simone Feisty Pants Miller."

"Don't start with me. I'll see you when you get here."

Clay showed up smelling of booze and pot. Disappointed, I suggested we hang out in the living room with the TV watching us as we caught up on old times. Clay passed on my offer of a snack because he was still full from an earlier dinner. I wanted to clarify whether it was simply dinner, or a dinner-date, but it was none of my business. We talked briefly before he fell sound asleep on my couch. I left him there and quietly went upstairs to my bed.

A few minutes later Clay crawled under the sheets and fell asleep for the rest of the night, polluting my room with noxious fumes. The stench of stale liquor escaped his nostrils with every breath he took. His sweaty ass lay drunk in my bed hoarding the sheets. I shook my head thinking, *Some people can't change. Clay is living . . . well . . . sleeping proof.* I wanted to shake the life out of him for being who he was. Sometimes I wished that rain had canceled the community carnival where we first met.

As the night wore on, I was restless with thoughts of Andy lodged deep in the back of my head. As the scripture goes, . . . *the mind controlled by the Spirit is life and peace.* Lying next to the same-ole Clay while thinking about disrespectful Andy proved that I wasn't fully committed to creating the peace that I wanted to experience within.

26

SPIRITUAL CONSTRUCTION

The alarm clock went off, followed by the telephone. I reached over Clay to take the call.

"Good morning. Can you hear me? It's Susan."

"No, Susan. My sense of hearing is still asleep. What is it?"

"Sorry to wake you. I thought you would be on your way out the door for church by now."

"I overslept. I'm going to the 11 o'clock service."

I was certain that my sister Susan hadn't called to find out what service I was attending. I got out of bed and walked to the bathroom waiting for Susan to tell me why she was really calling.

"I need a favor," Susan announced.

"How much is this favor gonna cost me?"

"I'm not asking to borrow money."

"Thank goodness because you still owe me from the last time I loaned you money. When can I expect to get my money back?"

"Simone, we should be even since you didn't offer to pay me for my time checking on your house while you were in Florida."

"Susan, please. Why would I pay you for something like that when I could have hired a security company to do a better job than you did? You and your husband still owe me $1,600 dollars for catching up your rent. Any chances of me seeing a fraction of that good deed today?"

"That's not why I called."

I sighed. "Susan, you're gonna need money again because Barry isn't reliable and you spend every dime you get picking up his slack."

"Isn't that what married people are supposed to do, have each other's back? Oh, wait! You're not even close to a marriage proposal because you're still dating Mr. Wrong. So you wouldn't understand."

"I'd rather be single and independent, than married to a broke bum like Barry."

"Shame on you badmouthing my husband and talking about going to church this morning."

I laughed, "I'm human and still under spiritual construction so all will be forgiven."

"If you say so. Listen," Susan said abruptly. "I called because Sasha and Monica are going to the amusement park tomorrow. Could you braid their hair for me?"

"Sure, I'll come over after church."

After showering, I discreetly poked my head into the bedroom and witnessed Clay wallowing in my bed and smelling my sheets. I was almost certain that I heard him say he missed Lady, too. I let the past live in the past, and finished dressing in the den so that Clay could roll back down memory lane in private.

27

BENT OVER

An hour later, freshly showered and dressed, I said good-bye to Clay and made my way to service. New Baptist had 600 members and counting, a sign of more lives being saved and more souls being touched. My hour of worship usually took place during the first service; it was early, mellow, and not as crowded as the second. I didn't have a choice that morning because I overslept.

Pastor Jenkins preaching the word of God was always a blessing. On any given Sunday, I gained clear perspective about my walk with Christ and rejected the harshness of hypocrisy that existed inside New Baptist; especially the holier-than-thou members who enlisted themselves as spiritual heroes. Their self-appointed duty was to go out into the community and beat so-called worldly people over the head with spiritual batons, but in the sanctuary, fellow members would be hard-pressed to get a quiet hello out of them.

I had witnessed blatant hypocrisy, promiscuity, infidelity, and bad attitudes—just to name a few unholy dispositions at New Baptist. The sanctuary, at times, was a rainbow of sin.

Sister so-and-so was telling it and Brother so-and-so was doing it. I concluded for some Sunday morning Christians, church was viewed as belonging to a club, an organization of some sort. Carrying the Bible didn't grant everyone access. The doors to those inner circles were political appointments for a privileged few. My good friend Cindy gave me her best spiritual advice yet: "Don't be discouraged by Man. Live for your Lord and your Lord only."

Amen to that, I thought as I entered the sanctuary.

Inside, New Baptist was jammed-pack with standing room only. I wandered around the vestibule for a seat. Portia and Denise were nowhere to be seen in the crowd of big, feathery hats gracing the heads of stylish Christians. An usher on duty gave me a program. I hugged my Christian Sister for making me feel welcome. After, she guided me down the tapered aisle towards the pulpit area. As I made my way to the middle of the pew, fellow worshippers too vain to wrinkle their see-me-outfits, didn't hurry to make room for me. The whole row of them gave a dismissive look, as though they had been forewarned: Satan has entered the building.

I cleared my throat and got specific with Christian authority. Using my library voice I asked, "May, I please take the seat in the middle that is not taken?"

A response came, however phony in nature.

"Sure. Come on in. Sit down. Sit down. It's a little tight, though. The ushers couldn't find you a seat in the vestibule?" One had the audacity to ask.

My eyebrows shot up in disbelief. I put my Bible in the placeholder on the back of the pew directly in front of my seat; afterward I addressed Miss Hoity-Toity, "Is that where you would prefer to sit?" She was stunned to silence.

Pastor Jenkins approached the pulpit wearing a black floor length dress that hung loosely around her body. Near the altar there was a crucifix nailed to the wall, candles burning on the offering table, potted plants on the mantel, and a backfill of rows to accommodate the choir.

The Word was going to be very deep and very real because I felt the spirit moving in my soul.

The Mass Choir, clad in red and black robes, made a spirited entrance with tambourines in hand, and powerful voices praising the Lord for waking them up. After Selection A, they immediately went to their seats.

A small voice squealed from the balcony, "Can a *Divo* have everyone's attention please?"

Everything stopped moving except the fan blades twirling in rapid motion above our heads. Flames flickered on the candles. I'd immediately recognized Ritchie's voice. But I couldn't believe my ears or eyes as he sashayed in between the pews, destined for the altar. He stopped midway, pushed his butt out, and double snapped his fingers while simultaneously turning his body so that his front was facing the congregation.

What was up with the super model runway act? Ritchie had me wondering. I knew his Divo antics could be extreme, but church was no place to act them out.

Deacon Brown approached Ritchie, "What's on your heart this morning, young man?"

Ritchie batted his eyes, and started fanning his face. Then he dropped himself to the floor and started hollering, and crying, "Nobody loves me. Nobody loves me."

Deacon Brown attempted to help Ritchie up off the floor. Ritchie growled, "I'm okay. I'm okay. Let go of me. Let go of me damn it!" He yelled getting up.

Pastor Jenkins had seen enough.

"Young man, is there something you want to say? If not, I will ask you to take a seat so we can get the service underway."

Ritchie started sobbing, "I need love. We all need love. Love makes the world go around." Then he held his arms over his head, and started spinning in circles until he collapsed. Deacon Brown, with the help of two male members, carried Ritchie into a nearby room. That was the last I saw of him.

Pastor Jenkins spoke into the microphone, "Good morning, church. Before I introduce today's sermon, let us do right by that brother and pray for him. Amen?"

The congregation said, "Amen."

"Bow your heads, please. Lord, help our brother find peace in his time of personal anguish. Guide him in all that he does. Keep him on the path of righteousness. Heal his heart. Calm his mind. And Give him the strength to claim victory over the enemy. Amen."

Without delay, Pastor Jenkins segued into her prepared sermon.

"Today, I am going to do something very different and preach from my heart so you better get ready for the truth—it's hard and heavy. Is that okay with you?"

The congregation responded, "Preach!"

"My sermon today is titled: Bent Over. Simply put, we only see our physical disabilities because we mask the emotional turmoil of our inner demons. It's time to stop living a lie Christians. Don't just hear the word, live it!"

The sanctuary got pin drop quiet. Pastor Jenkins went on to touch some nerves calling out marital affairs, abuse, gossip, and messy Christians. Addicts didn't dodge her spiritual bullet, either. Telling-it-like-it-was, Pastor Jenkins encouraged addicts to seek counseling, be it for shopping, sex, gambling, alcohol, or drugs. Some members looked at their neighbor like she wasn't talking about them—even I was guilty of at least one of those addictions.

Pastor Jenkins ministered to the congregation in many ways, offering rations of daily bread and spiritual solutions to solve our problems. She was no therapist, but she was uniquely qualified to counsel the congregation.

With her head bopping from side to side, and finger pointing out towards the congregation, hot under her spiritual collar Pastor Jenkins shouted, "Women get married, or close up shop and send your non-committal lover packing! And wives, fawn over your husbands just as much as you dote on friends that ain't keeping a roof over your head. Jezebels, leave married men alone. Two-timing, ungrateful husbands, go home to your faithful wives!" she preached. "Punching bags, leave your abusive relationships and let your abuser wrestle with his own *damn* demons! Devoted Christians, turn a deaf ear to Messy Christian's who gossip and stir the pot of you-know-*what*. Experience has taught me, if they're catty and telling someone else's business, when you stop kissing their behinds they're gonna tear you down, too! And you had better be leery of the ones doing all the talking on social media, especially if they ain't talking about the graveyard of skeletons buried in their own backyard. Woo!" She shouted, fanning herself. "And another thing, you better keep messy folk out your house because they've been known steal joy, too."

Members jumped to their feet to encourage Pastor Jenkins.

"Preach!"

"You better say it!"

"Can I testify?"

"Saints." Pastor Jenkins paused and took a deep breath. "Before I get back to my sermon, turn with me to Psalms 41. Verse 6. Say Amen when you find it. " While Pastor Jenkins waited to hear Amen, she sipped from a glass of water and then took a deep breath.

"Take your time. Take your time." A member advised.

Pastor Jenkins picked up where she had left off in her sermon. "The Scripture says, *Whenever they come to see me, they speak falsely, while their hearts gather slander; then they go out and spread it abroad.* If you can relate shout amen."

The congregation shouted, "Amen!"

"Church, distance yourselves from anyone that is not working for the greater good of mankind to spread peace and love. Cast all that ugliness aside, rebuke Satan in the name of Jesus and live a righteous life! That is what God wants you to do. That's what I expect to see in New Baptist as I stand in for Pastor Cox while he recovers from surgery. I am going to hold you accountable to the teachings of the Bible because the Good Book says, *In all your ways acknowledge him, and he will make your paths straight.* You can't walk your spiritual journey alone. You've gotta *leeeeeeannnnnnnnn* on Him in the good, bad, and so-so times!" Pastor Jenkins shouted leaning on the pulpit to emphasize the point of trusting God to be a spiritual pillar of support. Then she stood up straight, did a quick and loud clap before breaking into her favorite song. "Come on church! Y'all gonna sing with me today. Here we go, "My redeemer has saved me from sin." She sang then stopped and

said, "Y'all know that song, right? If you don't, it's called *Free.*
Now let me hear those angelic voices locked in Satan's chamber cry out to be free. The Lord will hear you and He always
comes when you call. She started singing again. *My soul is
awakened...*" Pastor Jenkins's voiced soared above the congregation who was now standing on its feet immersed in the rap-
ture of glory.

Her spirit-rousing delivery came close to moving me to
dance and declare I want to be free. But I gave twenty percent
instead.

28

MR. WRONG

I finished braiding Sasha and Monica's hair in record time. I couldn't take another minute of spoiled rotten Dallas wanting to climb all over me like he was a bird and I was his tree. Susan catering to her lazy, freeloading, husband Barry to a ridiculous degree of overkill pushed me out the door faster.

While I prepared to leave, Barry was unusually nice to me as I gathered up my hair-styling tools, and packed up my church clothes and shoes that were still strewn over the couch after I had changed into comfortable sweats, and a t-shirt.

"Let me get the door for you." He said, grinning a little too much for me to trust his unusual act of chivalry. Barry knew that I didn't care much for him. When I first met him I didn't like the fact that he was a reformed alcoholic given that Susan was on a slippery slope recovering from her own addiction. Then his seasonal employment habits started to affect my pockets since Susan always seemed to fall behind on bills and then depend on me for a cash bail out. Saying no to

Susan's financial needs would have been denying my nieces and nephew the stability they needed. But it seemed the more I helped the less Barry tried to find stable employment. When he worked long enough to earn six months salary, he spent it on expensive clothes and cologne instead of paying the bills or paying me back.

Standing near the door Barry tried to make conversation with me.

"You know, you should really considering Hair College. You do great work."

"Hair College exists?" I asked, honestly confused because I had never heard Cosmetology School referred to as Hair College.

"Yeah, you know where you go for formal hair training to get a license to perm, cut, and all that other stuff women do to make themselves look good and feel good."

"Oh, you mean—" Susan cleared her throat cutting me off. I stopped myself when I saw her eyes begging me not to embarrass Barry. "Cosmetology School is not on my short list of goals. But thanks for appreciating what I enjoy doing as a hobby."

"Don't mention it. Say, are you still waiting for Mr. Wrong to act right?"

"Excuse me, rude ass?"

Susan almost slipped and fell throwing her body between us. "Look you two. No arguing, and definitely not in front of the kids. Monica, Sasha, and Dallas go to your rooms."

"You *two?*" I repeated. "Susan why are you putting his rudeness off on me? He went from cozying up with small talk to insulting me. That's why I don't come over here."

"Simone, don't take it to heart. I was just asking because Susan mentioned the other day how she thought you and Andy break up to make up too much."

Rolling my eyes at Susan, I turned to face her. "Really?"

"Simone, we were just talking, that's all." She said, trying to keep the peace.

"Funny you have time to discuss me and not the Help Wanted ads. Let me get out of here before I say something God won't forgive me for saying."

"Don't leave mad," Susan pleaded.

"I'm not mad, but I'm not leaving without answering his question." I then turned to face Barry. "Mr. Right might come along before you and Susan can scrape up the money that she borrowed to pick up *your* slack. At least my Mr. Wrong works. Too bad you don't have a job to keep your bills paid."

"All right Simone," Susan said pulling me to the door. "You've said enough. Call me later when you're not upset."

"No! You can call me when you think an apology is in order." I said pulling out of her grasp and turning back to Barry who had a smirk on his face. "Better yet Susan, call me when your *huuussssssband* gets and keeps a job for one year." I then stepped outside and slammed the door behind me.

❧

As soon as I got one foot in the house, the telephone rang. Curious if it was Susan calling to apologize, I answered without hesitation.

"Hello."

"Please. Don't hang up. It's me."

I couldn't believe it was Andy on the line.

"Me?" I repeated. "Andy, you don't have that privilege anymore. State your first name when you call my house."

"Sweetheart, I didn't call to fight with you."

"You could've fooled me. Your fist sure felt like socking it to me a couple days ago. What do you want?"

"Look, I'm just calling to ask if you would like to go see a movie."

"Absolutely not."

"Why? We can go out to dinner after and talk things over."

"And then following the movie, dinner, and throwing back a few mixed drinks, you're gonna expect me to thank you with the sexy pussy I've got between my legs. Nice try. But, no thanks."

"Why are you always bitching at me? I screwed up. I'm willing to do whatever it takes to make things right."

"Mr. Wrong, you can never make things right because you're not right, you're selfish and disrespectful."

"Simone, you think you're so per fect, don't you? Well guess what, you're not. You're nothing but a bougie bitch! I don't need you either. There are plenty women who can give me what I want."

"Well, if I have to be a bitch to get respect, then bitch I am. I'd rather be a bitch, than your whore. Good riddance!"

I hung up before another word could roll off his malicious tongue. Bickering with Andy left me emotionally drained and dehydrated. I purified my soul with a glass of ice water just as the telephone rang again. The answering machine played the outgoing greeting:

> Caller, you have one minute to record your message. Keep it short and sweet, here comes the beep.

To my surprise, Shelly's voice came through the box. Since the reunion, we had built a rapport and a strong bond that made me want to trust her. I quickly picked up the phone.

"Shelly, I'm home."

"Why are you screening your calls?"

Before I could answer her question, my call-waiting signal beeped.

"Hang on Shelly." I clicked over. "Speak."

It was Andy.

"Simone, would you please hear me out? I have a proposition to make. Would you consider taking a little time away from one another to see what else is out there? I'm willing if you are."

My blood was boiling like hot tomato soup.

"Andy, what kind of fool do you take me for? I have ironclad proof that you already know what's out there. That's another reason I won't have sex with you any more. Does burgundy hair mean anything to you?"

"Hair? What burgundy hair? Sweetheart, stop being difficult."

"I found strands of it on your pillowcase a year ago."

"Sweetheart, a year ago?" Andy chuckled. "I honestly don't know where that could have come from. Maybe it got caught in my sheets at the laundry mat. That's the only thing I can think of that makes sense. But it wasn't from another woman. I enjoy you too much to risk losing what's between your legs."

"What the hell do you mean losing? You don't own my vagina!"

"I didn't mean it like that. I meant—"

"I don't care what you meant and I don't believe your story. It's over. Call me again and I will slap you with a restraining order for harassment."

"Simone, you'd do that to me knowing how much I love you?"

"Correction! I know how much you love to take what you want with no regards to how I feel. Don't call my house again."

I hung up on Andy and got back to Shelly. She sensed something was wrong.

"Sis, do you want to pray about it?"

"Oh, it's not that serious."

"Okay, remember that I'm here to listen."

"Thanks for the moral support. Now, let's talk about your upcoming visit to Boston. First, I must warn you, my neighbors are nosy. It's a real Peyton Place, so don't be surprised if my neighbors spy on your every move."

"Well, in that case, I will pack my spiritual boxing gloves to do battle on Satan's turf."

We laughed then prayed to stay blessed, not stressed, and hung up. The time had come to crack the egg and swim in my own yolk for a change. My preordained moment allowed me to emotionally break away from social drama, and put myself first. Walking away from confusion for a minute to clear my head revealed that life was not so bad after all. I truly wanted to welcome peace.

I reached for the *Mountain High, Valley Low* CD and fast-forwarded to track five, "In The Midst Of It All". I cranked the volume high, and let the music play while I danced to spiritual guidance.

About an hour of peace went by before Andy called trying to weasel his way out the doghouse.

"Sweetheart, can we talk?"

"Andy, you said what you had to say now hear what I have to say. The more you try to take from me, the more I will have to hold over your head standing before a judge." I forewarned.

A call beeped in. I clicked over without notice to Andy. It was Keisha.

"Simone, what are you doing cooped up in the house? Why aren't you out soaking up the sun with Andy?"

"We had a disagreement. He's back in the doghouse for good."

"You're upset. I'm sure you'll get over what ever he did and make up by next week. You always do."

"Not this time around."

"I think Andy really needs you, and he cares a lot about you and you care about him, too."

"Keisha, what makes you say that?"

"I hear it in your voice and if you two didn't love each other you wouldn't fight so much. Work it out because we all need somebody to grow old with."

"Does needing somebody mean putting them above my self-esteem?"

"Simone, I'm not saying that."

"Then what are you saying?"

"Look at the time you spent together. It's gotta mean something."

"It's a lot deeper than time spent together. Andy's presence has been a weight on my heart. All he wants to do is take what belongs to me. I feel like his selfish desires are holding me back from meeting someone who values a relationship, and not just the 'sexy pussy' between my legs."

Keisha giggled, "Way too much information. Anyway, have you thought about couple's therapy?"

"Therapy with my fickle boyfriend?"

"Yes. What's wrong with that?"

"Please don't make me hang up on you for talking nonsense."

"It was only a thought. I'd do it in a heartbeat."

"With a married wallet?"

"Ha ha ha. Very funny Simone."

"I'm not laughing."

"I'm curious, would you marry Andy?"

"No but I'm confident someday I will meet Mr. Right."

"While waiting, you're gonna get lonely and give into Andy."

"Keisha, a bad relationship is no cure for loneliness."

"Maybe not but..."

"What about you Keisha. Do you ever tire of laying on your back in five star hotels with a married wallet for designer shoes and rent money, while his wife ain't gotta put out to spend his paycheck, to qualify for his pension, and half of his net worth?"

"What I give Gordon is too good for him to walk away. Plus he's quite generous. You should see these bad ass Jimmy Choos I'm wearing today! They got me feeling like a million bucks."

"You're employed. Buy your own shoes."

"Simone you don't get it."

"Then help me understand you screwing a married man who wants to have unprotected sex. Speaking of, what about your condom dilemma. Is it on or off?"

"Bye Simone."

"Avoiding the topic answers the question."

"Why do you care?"

"I care because I'm your friend and I'm worried that you're putting yourself at risk for sexually transmitted infections, especially after you said he had a medical issue and then disappeared on you."

"He said it was a false alarm and apologized. "

"Never trust the words of a cheating husband."

Keisha moaned, "Simone."

"Anyway, if you give in to his wants, which disease will be your parting gift when Gordon is finished with you?"

"Good bye Simone."

Keisha hung up before I could say, "Condom on."My cell phone rang. "I picked it up to find Portia's number flashing on the screen.

I was glad to hear from her so I happily answered, "How's it going?"

"Eh." She said sadly.

"Just 'eh'?"

"Yeah. Wait a minute. I hear the bell.   That could be Lonnie."

"Why is he ringing the bell like a maniac?" I asked.

"I'm not moving fast enough I guess. Excuse me for a second. Who is it?" I heard Portia say in the background.

"Who do you think it is? If I had a key you wouldn't have to buzz me in!" Lonnie barked.

"Don't start with me. The door will be open when you get up here." Portia said before coming back on the line. "Simone, I'm back."

"Portia, you and Lonnie haven't been dating a year and he expects a *key* to your condo?"

"He can expect all he wants but I'm not at that point of trust yet."

"Has he hit you again?"

"He pushed me but claimed he was only trying to get by to leave."

"He comes off as a hothead. Have you been back to church together since meeting at Bible study?"

"Building my Blush Cosmetics client base has been time consuming. I know that's no excuse but I try to get him to read scripture at home, but he blows it off."

"He blows what off?" Lonnie asked angrily in the background. "Are you talking about me? Give me that phone. Who is this?"

"It's Simone. How are you?"

"Portia is busy," he barked and abruptly hung up.

EPILOGUE

L onnie's volatile behavior validated my reasons for getting rid of Andy, which reminded me, Internet Romeo owes me a response. So I took a few minutes to log onto my new computer, skimmed online newspapers, and checked the Dow Jones Industrial Average. My inbox was flooded but I bypassed messages in favor of Romeo's response.

From: InternetRomeo@gp.drama
To: Simmy@gp.drama
Subject: REMEDY 4 SD

Message:

It took you FOREVER to write back; I wondered what interesting things would enter our conversation. I'm disappointed to hear that you DO have a boyfriend and that he's taking you for granted. I gave a lot of thought to your question. I think I can help.

Couples today don't take quality time to get to know each other beyond the bedroom. Chemistry revolves around the physical, and when we *do* get out of bed, we have nothing in common. Once the physical is removed, the only thing left: two discontent people who never thought to place an emphasis on spiritual compatibility.

A more direct answer to your question—you need to let go. Don't set yourself up to carry around a heavy heart for the rest of your life. If you MUST have a man, look for someone with compatible interests, values and goals, never settle.

I suggest you take some time out of your busy schedule to write this person a kind, honest note and keep in mind that it may cost you what little peace you have left. Sometimes a man finds it hard to let a good woman go. He expects to have her any time he feels; in his mind, it gives him validation and control, especially when he's at a recurring low point in his life. Take it from someone who's been there, and played the "poor me" card—men get a false sense of superiority when they gain control over a woman's mind, and body, but above all, her heart. Don't forget that *people will only treat you the way you allow them to treat you.* That said, women have to shoulder responsibility for how they allow men to treat them. Women give men too much recognition by stroking the manhood, and after serving their purpose, women get to wait around for hours, days, months and sometimes years until they are needed again.

YOU may not like what I'm about to say, but the law of physics says the seesaw-of-lust takes two to operate. Don't enable this person to make you a slave to his penis. Take charge. You come across as someone strong and determined. Judging you, of course, by the words you write; for all I know, you could be a card-carrying member of the emotionally impaired club. I doubt that very seriously, and please correct me if I'm wrong, a man also likes to know what he's dealing with. Anyway, I suggest you reassess your relationship, friendship, or booty call status with this person and determine if you can move on without him in your life, or at the very least, in your bed.

I'm going to be a man about it and tell you what you should already know—the Rules for Disengagement: Stop taking his calls, assuming you answer a couple for personal reasons. Don't answer when he shows up knocking at your front door or try creeping in through the back. Invest in a dildo or one better, claim celibacy, and say no more sheets! If his feelings for you are genuine, he will go away and let you live in peace. Now here comes the flip side, if he thinks of you as a good piece of ass, he will give you a million and one reasons why he needs you in his life. It's the "poor me syndrome". It's supposed to make you will feel remorseful and give ultimatums that won't last. On that note, you might have to be a royal *Babe In Total Control of Herself,* and seize the opportunity to tell him to go fuck himself.

P.S. Leaving should bring peace in mind.

From: Simmy@gp.drama
To: InternetRomeo@gp.drama
Subject: CURED!!!

Message:

What you said is a reflection of my attitude when I walked away from an ex-boyfriend with a cheating heart and a fast car. I deluded myself to thinking I was strong and tough until I started feeling like I wanted to love again. Not that I didn't desire to love, I didn't have the will because the feeling no longer existed within me. I guess I was in lust with the idea of love being on the horizon with this person. But it seems like my relationships were just fantasies that faded like the summer and left harsh reminders like the passing of a winter storm.

If someone had told me this thing called *Love* was going to be heavy on the heart, I would've dodged Cupid's arrow, and started learning to love me more a long time ago.

Thanks for the reality check! As Thomas Warfield once said: *The destination isn't in finding yourself. The destination is in the search.*

CLOSING REMARKS

Communicate with an open mind, listen with understanding, and find the courage to walk away from any situation that brings you emotional and physical harm. Above all, creating the peace that you want to experience starts from within. Love YOU more!

REFERENCE GUIDE

Waking up to a new day can mend your spirit and fill you with hope again.

Get in touch with your mind, body, and spirit. Research, seek professional guidance, and get the facts!

Alcoholics Anonymous
www.aa.org

Centers for Disease Control and Prevention
www.cdc.gov

Domestic Violence—The National Domestic Violence Hotline
1-800-799-SAFE
www.dvinstitute.org
www.ndvh.org

Self-awareness Resource (Blog)
http://tinybuddha.com/blog/
develop-self-awareness-and-improve-your-relationships/

Sexual Assault — RAINN (Rape, Abuse & Incest National Network)
https://www.rainn.org

Violence Against Women and Children (Facebook Page)
https://www.facebook.com/ViolenceAgainstWomenChildren

READING GROUP DISCUSSION GUIDE

1) After reading the title, did you immediately think sex?

2) Was there any one character that you could relate to personally? Why?

3) Why do you think Simone took so long to realize that Andy didn't love her?

4) Do you think Andy was sincere in his pursuit of Simone? Why? Why not? Did he deserve a second chance? Why? Why not?

5) Do you believe in second chances? Why? Why not?

6) Keisha finds fulfillment in dating a married man. Do you believe that material possessions are worth tolerating disrespect?

7) How do you think Keisha would function in a relationship with a single man?

8) Who should provide the condom in a relationship?

9) Do you think Portia will continue dating Lonnie? Why or why not?

10) Did you know that "1 in 4 women will experience domestic violence in her lifetime"?

11) Are you familiar with the relationship issues raised in the book? If so, which ones?

12) What topic(s) in the book resonated with you most: dating, domestic violence (verbal, emotional, and physical abuse), safe sex, family, friendship, or spiritual moments?

13) Do you think women rely on relationships to make them complete? Why? Why not?

14) Did the novel inspire you to be more attentive to your relationship or about how to choose a mate?

15) After reading this novel, how would you respond to this question: Are you being true to yourself?

16) The book was written to raise self-awareness. Do you think the author accomplished that objective?

If you have experienced any of the relationship scenarios in this novel, please feel free to share your story at: sh@sonyaharris.com

Like Facebook Author page: https://www.facebook.com/author_sonyaharris

Follow me on Twitter: @author_sonya

Like Facebook page: https://www.facebook.com/ViolenceAgainstWomenChildren

Sequel novel, *My Body Is Calling...* aims to raise health awareness. Copies of *My Body is Calling* ISBN: 978-0-9754458-2-2 can be ordered or purchased wherever books are sold.

Be light.

www.ingramcontent.com/pod-product-compliance
Lightning Source LLC
LaVergne TN
LVHW051056080426
835508LV00019B/1903